The Prime Law

The Prime Law

A Sinner's Guide to Democracy

D. P. Hendrickx

RESOURCE *Publications* · Eugene, Oregon

Resource Publications
An Imprint of Wipf and Stock Publishers
199 W. 8th Ave., Suite 3
Eugene, OR 97401

www.wipfandstock.com

PAPERBACK ISBN: 978-1-6667-7434-4
HARDCOVER ISBN: 978-1-6667-7435-1
EBOOK ISBN: 978-1-6667-7436-8

VERSION NUMBER 10/12/23

For Rosemary

Contents

Preface

MY SEARCH FOR THE answer began in the Old Testament Book of Job, at a time I was outside of myself looking in. A dark tornado of events had left my brain churning, rationalizing the irrational—for months. Somewhere in that chaos, a vague memory emerged: *the patience of Job*. I remembered hearing about that long-suffering character as a child. Patience. The word comforted me. From a calmer place, it beckoned me toward the Bible my mother, Lee, had received from my brother during her ordeal with bile duct cancer. One day her skin turned yellow. It was the only warning she had. That slow two-year descent spun me down—and her away.

I read Job, hard. As if they had a life and mind of their own, the words strangely pushed back, just as hard. Controlling words was a tool of my trade in the law, massaging them into place, gauging the efficacy of their spin. It was satisfying. It made reality more palatable. There was power in words. But this was different. Forcing my desired interpretation upon them caused the words to bounce off the page and disappear, along with the patience I longed for in their meaning.

My corporeal, reasoning brain was rejecting the spiritual. Such words were not understood with the brain, or with reason, but with one's heart—words meant not for interpretation but rather *consumption*. Only after consuming the words was their meaning revealed. The food was free. Tasting it, however, had a cost. The process was alien, uncomfortable. My heart had not been properly prepared to receive them.

I controlled nothing.

This was the whole point of Job, as well as the purpose of the exercise God intended for me. Satan was complaining to God that given the chance, Job, a righteous man, would curse God when faced with hardship. Knowing the strength of the man he created, and Satan's weakness, the omniscient God said, "Go for it." The father of cynics relieved Job of everything he had—his property, his children, his health—everything except his life, which God forbade. Life is, after all, the thing to which hardships adhere.

Despite Satan's bravado, Job, incredibly, still worshipped God: "Naked I came from my mother's womb, and naked I will depart. The LORD gave and the LORD has taken away; may the name of the LORD be praised."[1] Job's wife cruelly twisted the knife: "Are you still maintaining your integrity? Curse God and die!"[2] Now abandoned by his most intimate support, Job reproved, "Shall we accept good from God, and not trouble?"[3] His concession seemed weak. That was what my grief was telling me. Enough was enough. It was natural to fight back—survival of the fittest. Who would blame him—certainly not his faithless spouse? But my heart was telling me something else. His response was unnervingly real and true.

Some of Job's friends came to sit with him awhile in support. They did so in silence for a time, sharing the weight of his sorrow as good friends do. Even in their best intentions, however, they could not resist the temptation to pass judgment. Feeding his misery, they plied him with unwelcome, self-serving wisdom. The anguished man was alone. There, in that solitude and pain, God introduced me to Job—in a place no one else understood. We sat commiserating, staring together at the storm swirling about us.[4] Satan no doubt smiled at a good day's work. That is when he is at his best, when we are alone and vulnerable.

Job poured himself out to God. Why was all this happening? What had he done? God's treatment of Job seemed unfair, even capricious. Why does God permit evil to prosper but not the good? He had turned a blind eye to Job, as he had to me. My new friend was speaking for me. He marshaled his facts and demanded to make his case—and that God listen.[5] His defense was to hold up his righteousness against that of his fellow man as if to say, "God, compare me"; "I'm good"; "What more do you want?"

Yet something felt off. My rusty conscience sensed he had breached that hazy line between the righteous and the self-righteous. It was a call I, like Job's kibitzing friends, was not qualified to make. Why was I making

1. Job 1:21.
2. Job 2:9.
3. Job 2:10.
4. See Job 1:19.
5. See, e.g., Job 13:17–19; 23:3–5.

it? Who was I to judge a man whose loss I could barely comprehend? Did I know God better than Job did?

That was it . . . the "Oh" moment. The storm ebbed, just enough for me to glimpse the hypocrisy and arrogance that God, in his infinite wisdom, was revealing in me. While I had always believed in God, I had absolutely no idea who he was. He was a creation of my own comfort—my own needs and desires. More disconcerting was the revelation that in defining him, I had defined myself. I was God. He was merely an approving reflection of my own image, a fast friend constantly reassuring me that, for all intents and purposes, I was a good man—at least as good as the next. And that was enough.

The shocking revelation was that the identity I chose for myself and presented to the world was irrelevant to the God who created me. He knew exactly who I was, but that had nothing to do with how I saw myself. That fiction stood between us. A lifetime of comparing myself to others, of nurturing a false image, was exposed. It was not other people against whom I should have been comparing myself—it was him. As that self-deception crumbled away, a profound shame welled up in its place, the pain of clarity. To truly know ourselves, we must first know God.

I created nothing.

As with Job, that metric was real, not some theoretical exercise in comparative or relative morality. All I could do was shut my mouth and accept it. There was no defense, no argument. It was not the storm—Satan's distraction—against which I was helpless. It was God. Against that perfection, who was I? A hypocrite: *that* was my true identity. His perfection exposed my imperfection, my hypocrisy. In measuring myself against others, I had simply donned a phony crown, vainly usurping this King's perfection, hiding my own sins behind those of others. There was always someone else worse than me. And I was more than happy to point it out. Shifting accountability was an important tool in the lawyer's bag of skills.

I was *not* God.

Nor was I Job. I could not even claim a portion of his righteousness as my own. There was no one on earth more blameless and upright than Job.[6] God chose him for a reason, to make a point that even Satan in all his evil genius could not comprehend. Job's great faith, even though he lost sight of it for a time in his distress, was the strength and power of God himself.

Like it or not, we are not always privy to God's plan. Good people suffer—for no apparent human reason. What matters is our response to it.

6. See Job 1:8—2:3

Do we become victims, blaming him or others for our trials, or do we work through them in faith, relying on his strength, growing stronger ourselves in the process? Do we give up and die, or do we live? Had it been me, I might have taken Job's wife's advice and been done with it. Satan would have proved God false.

At length God confirmed his true nature to Job. As he did, he revealed it to me. Any prerogative Job claimed for himself in his own sense of righteousness was nothing compared with that of his God's. All creation was designed, made, and directed by his will, for his greater purpose. We are but one part of that eternal, boundless creation, which he loves, nurtures, judges, disciplines, and even uses as his justice demands, just as he used Job—*and* Satan—to make his point and establish his truth: it is God's grace that sustains us all.

After God finished revealing to Job their vast differences, the humbled man replied:

> I know that you can do all things; no purpose of yours can be thwarted. You asked, "Who is this that obscures my plans without knowledge?" Surely I spoke of things I did not understand, things too wonderful for me to know. You said, "Listen now, and I will speak; I will question you, and you shall answer me." My ears had heard of you but now my eyes have seen you. Therefore I despise myself and repent in dust and ashes.[7]

In the end, I learned that it was not patience that Job's ordeal produced in him; it was *humility*. He had been stripped down to his bare essence—not the embellished man, the sum of all his labors and desires, but the one God had created. Only then could he truly hear what God had to say. The search for God's truth comes at a cost. The price for tasting that truth was no less than one's self. In that submission Job now understood who God was—and who he himself was. He was a better, wiser man for it. Job relinquished his self-made crown—his image and sovereignty—to God.

Out of the chaos in his life, order was reestablished, a higher truth applicable to all things. My arrogance and lack of faith obscured that wisdom, my ability to see the words on that page, to hear the truth, to know God. Words which firmly, persistently said to me: *Be quiet, and judge yourself.*

God restored Job. There was hope for me.

The Book of Job reveals that preserving our temporal existence is not God's endgame. It is merely a backdrop for the spiritual battle being

---

7. Job 42:2–6.

waged between good and evil—inside of ourselves and out. There is a vast difference between God's morality and the relative morality we create for ourselves—a morality based not in God's love, but in *self*. Power, influence, wealth, and image count for nothing. The hate we proffer to keep this world divided proves it, designed to keep us laser-focused on ourselves and our differences. By it we deceive and are being deceived, diverting our eyes from God's true endgame—our eternal reconciliation—*our unity*.

Job's journey in rediscovering his humility models our earthly paths through that battle, to unity with God, and hence with one another. His story is one of shedding that which keeps us bound to this earth, of coming to terms with who we really are, of subordinating our autonomy to God, of preparing our hearts to hear his spiritual truth. True unity is a spiritual matter. The spiritual language of unity is understood not with the mind, but with the heart; not with reason, but with humility and love. It is a hard lesson in a self-interested, material world.

I would later understand more clearly the scope of that humility and love in the life, sacrificial death, and resurrection of Jesus Christ. Although I did not know it at the time, the Book of Job looked forward to Christ's New Testament work of reconciliation and unity in the physical world. Our unity in Christ was God's endgame. It was the only absolute truth I had ever come to understand and accept. The reason I accepted it was that as measured against the purity and perfection of that sacrifice, I was completely lacking. What had changed was that now, after touching the bottom, I knew it.

In God's perfection, there is no storm.

The cost of providing me that clarity was immeasurable. As Job himself could testify, God spared no expense in doing so. It cost Job everything he held dear. It cost Christ his life. It cost God his son, and countless others too, patriots of the faith. That was the cost of being freed from the constraints of my ego and ignorance—of infusing the perfect into the imperfect. What was the cost to me? Someone else paid the price. Who would do such a thing and why?

I was loved and not alone.

Unpacking that humility is the journey of a Christian. It is wrapped around many things: love, mercy, grace, even law and judgment. Yet that one seminal concept—that absolute perfect humility, and my subordination to it, changed everything. It was a new reference point from which I saw myself and the world around me. Acknowledging it was not a negative thing. Rather, it was a new foundation, the beginning of a positive order in my life informing all that I perceived, putting all of life's complicated relationships into appropriate context.

Despite what many would (and do) consider weakness, my submission to this higher truth, this faith, was, as it was for Job, the power of God's love working in me. Not just for my sake, but for the sake of all those whose lives would intersect with mine. The ability to see everyone as I saw myself, as an equal creation of God, was a consequence of that humility. That "equality" stemmed not from fallible human law, but from God's infallible love.

With this new clarity it seemed that all of today's demands for social justice were, like Job's demands of God, nothing but attempts to reacquire the equality and independence that is already abundantly ours in our submission to that higher spiritual truth—*God's Prime Law*: to love God with all our hearts, and to love others as we love ourselves. In that love we are all perfectly equal. That superior truth—the unchanging Law of God—is impervious to human error or manipulation. Our mutual submission to it, as his creations, is indeed the ultimate equalizer. In that equality is true freedom. In that freedom we can all unite.

Humility was the answer. Unity in Christ is the way.

That one revelation changed everything. It was a new path forward, lifting me up and out of the storm, providing a bird's eye view of the disunity in my life and its effect on those around me. We are—each of us, without exception—complicit in this nation's disunity. That disunity is not simply a function of race, color, sex, religion, politics, or wealth. It is a function of something we *all* share in common, an innate need to manipulate and misuse those things to promote our self-interests or identities. What was the effect of that revelation on my worldview? That which motivates our thoughts, our perceptions, or our social and political biases influences our relationships with others—for good and bad.

For this writer that motivation came down to the ability, or willingness, to accept the existence of an *absolute truth*, a superior ideal or morality over which I had no control, one not limited or defined by my imperfect human reason. That willingness stemmed from the certain knowledge of having received from God a perspective on life—and death—that I could not possibly have conceived on my own. In that receipt I knew, without doubt, that God existed and that he loved me.

My hope for a better future now resided inside that superior ideal, in a perfect God, perfect love, and his perfect Law. My understanding about the effects of that ideal on our loss of individual and national unity developed over time, as did my faith. Faith is the long process of applying God's perfection to an imperfect life. Repairing our national disunity depends not on external political or social change, but on the internal process of rediscovering our individual humility and applying it daily to our lives and our relationships with others.

In the search for real truth, people are starving for unity in the storm we call government. That government is, after all, a series of human relationships. Amidst that storm we are witnessing the decline of our republican form of democracy and the freedoms it guarantees. Our egotistical demand for external change in others, rather than internal self-change, fuels our national disunity, impacting all of our relationships, including those comprising government. The greatest enemy of our national unity, our democracy, is our own vanity.

The Prime Law is this writer's perspective on that loss of individual humility and resulting national disunity. It goes to a place few willingly go and fewer truly understand—into the contentious fissure between church and state, Christianity and democracy. It frames that division as a battle between absolute truth and relativism, one enabled by the eighteenth-century Enlightenment movement and instilled into our nascent democracy.

While providing colonial America liberal support for freedom of thought and religious exercise, that same philosophy ironically provided justification for separating morality from God's divinity, thereby relativizing the two parts of God's Prime Law. Morality was deemed a function of our human reason—not God's superior love. No longer was that divine love integral to loving ourselves or loving others. Fueling the tension between our self-interest and our love for others, that separation has weakened our resolve to self-regulate, fostering the need for a larger, more intrusive government to fill the void created by our lack of personal accountability.

Unlike the self-interest of identity politics currently defining that government, the Christian's identity and truth is found not in one's self or image, but inside a substantive relationship of love with God, the same God who provides us our ultimate freedom and equality. That relationship strengthens the love we share with others and our ultimate accountability to them. The dynamics of that relationship reveal, however, an uneasy paradox: that our true accountability, freedom, and equality—our democracy—arise from *submission*, a willingness to submit to a higher absolute truth, the Law of God—a more perfect humility.

Our path to unity lies not in restructuring or dismantling our democracy, but in our willingness to submit to that higher unalterable truth, restructuring ourselves and our relationships using the perfect humility and love of Jesus Christ as the template. That humility and love are the Spirit behind God's Prime Law. Infusing that Spirit into our temporal law fortifies our secular justice. By repairing the rift between divinity and morality, we repair not only the relationships comprising government and the laws it produces, but the individual's voluntary subordination to it. Our willingness to submit to God provides the means for submitting to each other and, hence, to our democratic rule of law.

It is hoped that this work points the reader to that path. On the way you will face some uncomfortable truths about yourself and your nature, as did Job (and this writer). Finding that truth is not a comfortable journey. It is not an exercise in self–affirmation. It requires a hard look at painful things—and making difficult decisions. And along the way, we are asked to cede our imperfect individual sovereignty to a perfect God—a fundamental transfer of trust. That was Job's journey. It is ours as well. You should close this essay with a clearer understanding of that trust, our relationship to God, and how it beneficially shapes our relationship with others. Understanding the fundamentals of that connection informs our perspective of political theory, law, and the interaction between faith and democracy.

Finally, I pray that you might consider the real potential for a more perfect relationship with Jesus Christ, the Prime Law's living icon. For that is the key to forming a more perfect union.

Introduction

When the foundations are being destroyed,
what can the righteous do?

—Psalm 11:3

Amicable debate and decorum in politics and media are dead, collateral damage in our national civil war of competing self-interests. If the smoke from the battlefield ever clears, we will find that this nation has devolved into something strangely unfamiliar, less American, less cohesive, and certainly less free than that envisioned by our founders. It is a gloomy, cynical place where the future is uncertain and the past merely a constant reminder of our victimization and failure.

Despite its pejorative shade today, being an "American" used to mean something positive and good. While the totality of that good may, at times, have been hard to define, it had, despite our individual differences and experiences, a common soul or spirit, a higher ideal, which meaningfully informed our equality, freedom, and justice. It was not a selfish pride. It was a collective or cooperative pride in being a part of something *greater than ourselves*—something inexorably moral and true. Despite those individual circumstances, we could all freely unite in that higher ideal, one that, for almost two hundred and fifty years, had inspired millions of people from all over the world to travel here seeking a better life.

But yesterday's leftover national pride is now today's hash of isms and phobias, angrily prepared and served up by those bent on disparaging the principles upon which this unique nation was cast. Along with our

1

morning coffee, we are all waking up to the sad headline that this nation's greatness was a lie. Our efforts over those last two hundred and fifty years? Meaningless. Duped were all those millions who left the poverty and despair of their home countries behind, only to find they had merely traded one corrupt nation for another. Who could ever have imagined that the sincere faith and patriotism that gave birth to and sustained this nation would today become the stuff of right-wing extremism? Or that the gifts flowing from our democracy were irreparably marred by systemic racism? The rational is now irrational. Civility has fallen into rancor. The world seems upside down.

Amid the divisive hatred and partisanship of that war—in the battle for our true identity as individuals and as a nation—our unique democracy struggles to survive. The common spirit of our nation and democracy, which should rightfully transcend all self-interest, has been defamed and suppressed by that victimization and failure.

The answer? Since we cannot change ourselves, our nature, why not simply change the system to conform to that nature? There are those who, unfortunately, feel that democracy has failed to solve the issues that perennially divide us regarding race, sex, economics, climate, and faith. Give government greater power to force compliance from the individual. We have proved our inability, or at least unwillingness, to control ourselves, to self-regulate. While true freedom is, ultimately, to be free from governmental compulsion, in our immaturity and lack of wisdom, it seems that we are unable to handle that freedom. Time and again, in exercising that freedom, we each invariably choose ourselves and our self-interest at the expense of others.

The truth, however, is that the issues dividing us are by no means specific to this nation, its history, or our democracy. They have marked the entirety of human existence. To denigrate this nation's great accomplishments as a result is to merely avoid the much larger problem, the reason for it all: our unbridled self-interest or sin. At best our vanity lies in thinking that changing the system will change the hearts of the individuals within it. It will not. At worst it acknowledges that we cannot change, and, therefore, the only thing we can do is grab power and control the chaos below. We are romanced by the fiery rhetoric of the former only to realize too late the exorbitant cost in freedom of the latter.

Still, we refuse to admit the complicity of our self-interest in those failures because in our vanity we cannot admit those failures in ourselves.

The sins of others are always worse than our own. We are content to end the inquiry into the human condition with those comparisons. To accept personal accountability for them, however, is to go further and admit our own need to change, to do better. And this we are not willing to do unless external forces compel us to do so. To affect real change, there must be a fear of consequences—*the force of law*. Unfortunately, demanding change to our form of government, or the secular laws and regulations it produces, will never address the root of that self-interest, the *individual's* sinful heart. How complex our lives have become because of that self-interest.

Those lives interweave to create the fabric of society. The character of each of those individual lives determines its ultimate strength and integrity. Does the individual possess a character for truth and doing what is right, or for lying and doing what is wrong? It sounds simple enough, even naïve. But the good vs. evil question has become so banal that we are numb to it. In that struggle for image and power, the difference has become irrelevant. Over time we have lost the desire to distinguish between the two. In fact, we weaponize that lack of distinction through propaganda and censorship in order to manipulate others, rendering national unity an impossible goal. In the failure of each one of us to confront that one question about ourselves, we are losing our internal compass and sense of order in what amounts to a fearful moral evolution.

The survival of our democracy—our freedom and unity—depends on our ability to do just that, to honestly assess ourselves. How do we under-stand the difference between good and bad? C.S. Lewis, Oxford and Cam-bridge educator, and author of the famed *Narnia* series, reasoned that "evil is a parasite. . . . All the things which enable a bad man to be effectively bad are in themselves good things—resolution, cleverness, good looks, exis-tence itself."[1] Lewis prefaced this observation about evil with brilliant logic:

> If "being good" meant simply joining the side you happen to fancy, for no real reason, then good would not deserve to be called good. So we must mean that one of the two powers is actually wrong and the other actually right.
>
> But the moment you say that, you are putting into the uni-verse a third thing in addition to the two Powers: some law or standard or rule of good which one of the powers conforms to and the other fails to conform to. But since the two powers are judged by this standard, then this standard, or the Being who made this standard, is farther back and higher up than either of them, and he

---

1. Lewis, *Mere Christianity*, 35–36.

will be the real God. In fact, what we meant by calling them good and bad turns out to be that one of them is in a right relation to the real ultimate God and the other in a wrong relation to Him.[2]

Thus good and bad are measured not against each other, but against God's higher standard. Lewis was pointing to a universal constant or truth—that good and evil are inextricably tied together.[3] Evil is a perversion of the good. That perversion is sin. In our sin a perfect God—a greater truth—is revealed. Good must be applied in order to be fulfilled. It requires an act. That act requires a motivation. That motivation, or reason, is the thing to which parasitic evil clings, the "wrong power." It is a part of us all. In our relative society, however, we are reluctant to distinguish between the two out of self-interest, apathy, or fear of causing offense.

Yet real character will always be defined by our ability to discern the difference, and a willingness to accept personal accountability for the decisions we make in light of those differences. As Lewis demonstrates, there must be an ultimate, unchangeable rule for measuring good and bad. That rule is the Law of God. By that Law we measure the quality of our actions—comparing ourselves not to other people, but to him.

The truth is that in the end, as a nation and a republic, regardless of race, color, creed, or sex, we all stand or fall together. Only after each one of us acknowledges the rule and thus accepts personal accountability, first for ourselves, and then for the state of this nation, can we unite together and meaningfully address the issues that affect us all. Therein we recapture our lost humility.

THE DEMAND FOR CONFORMANCE— SELF-IDENTITY AND SIN

Democracy is a tool. It works only if properly used—with humility and accountability. The truth and morality that were once the heart and soul of that democracy, the very things that set it apart from all other forms of government, are no longer fixed higher ideals applicable to us all, but rather relative marketing brands, ever-changing creations of our own design as we each strive to define ourselves and the world around us.

2. Lewis, *Mere Christianity*, 34.

3. See Rom 7:21: "So I find this law at work: Although I want to do good, evil is right there with me."

More than gloomy and cynical, it is, as a result, a chaotic world in which truth and morality now begin and end with the individual, expressed in the myriad elements we feel best empower us or best represent our desired outward image or persona. The war for survival of the fittest now rages on in the divisive competition between personal agendas or brands.

But mere expression of that brand or image is not the underlying problem—it never has been—for that is our constitutional right. Rather, it is the *demand* that others subscribe and conform to that image, and that government, by force of law, compels that subscription regardless of any consideration of morality or reciprocal rights. Self-interest demands a form of government that provides for that control, as if that identity alone confers upon us our inalienable rights. While it may be our secular right to self-determine, that identity, however, should not itself confer upon us any additional right or power to force others to conform to it. One is free to think and believe as they wish—and act accordingly within the limits of the law. But one is not free to compel thoughts and beliefs in another.

For example, to the believing Christian, the spiritual being is as real as the physical being, and together (as in Jesus Christ) they are one. That union, or identity, defines in part who they are. The Christian would even argue that this identity is not a choice but rather an intrinsic part of their nature as a creation of God, and a gift of his grace. That union, and its source in God's love, influences the Christian's understanding of morality, and thus the nature of their relationship with others. Even so, they cannot force others to accept that union and thus identify as Christians. Nor should they.

Regardless of one's self-definition, our Constitution recognizes our freedom from conformance by securing the freedom of thought and religion—whatever that may be—even the freedom of "no thought" or "no religion." No one should be forced to conform to a concept of identity that provides no structure or rules whatsoever for defining it apart from those an individual might, in their own mind, create. Self-identity becomes a secular moral issue when we attempt to force that construct on someone else.

In a true democracy the error of such a demand is obvious at once. If self-determination is our mutual right, the insecure demand that others subscribe to that construct or determination violates that right. In other words, we are not equally free to "self-determine." Like being compelled to adhere to a particular religion, faith, or political ideology, we are forced to incorporate another's chosen identity or image as part of our own.

That forced assimilation also requires that one concur in and support another's relative view of morality at the core of that identity. If not, contrary·opinion must be censored, silenced—by force of law if necessary. Enslaved by another's identity, the slave is no longer free to identify as truly free. No one has the right to force another to accept one's choice as being ultimately moral. Our right to dissent arises in the face of such undemocratic demands, a right upon which this nation was built. Dissent, rationally and peacefully expressed, has the power to change minds and change law. That is the true power of democracy.

Under secular law, we should all have the same right to "determine" or even "not determine." Such a rule, if it is to be a fair rule, must apply equally to everyone, or not at all. Otherwise, we invoke it simply as a means of coercion and control. Therein our constitutionally protected freedoms of religion, speech, association, and due process suffer. In the larger sense our freedom, equality, and justice all suffer—at the hands of those bent on destroying the very things that unite us all, the foundations of our democracy.

It is argued that our true identity, power, and unity are not found in the relative images we create for ourselves as expressions of our god-like autonomy—in manipulating or creating our own realities. Nor is our identity found in the groups or movements we cling to seeking support and security. To the extent that our personal image informs the group, or vice versa, that self-creation is a form of idolatry, as if those images alone justify our existence, supplying ultimate purpose and meaning in our lives. Like most idols, the external image rarely reflects the inner truth. In our pride we become slaves to those divisive individual or group identities, and in the process hostile to opinions or beliefs that contradict that identity.

Rather than in a self-created *image*, that identity must be derived from a common higher good, or law, to which we *all* submit, one that defines our mutual equality, freedom, and justice. For the believing Christian that identity, as mentioned above, is found not in an *image*, but in a *relationship* of love with God (the "good")—as his creation—realized in our love for others (the "good fulfilled").

It is beautifully expressed in God's Prime Law: "Love the Lord your God with all your heart and with all your soul and with all your mind. . . . Love your neighbor as yourself."[4] Regardless of any individual differences we may have, that love *is* God's truth. Inside that truth our common freedom, equality, and unity are defined, all thriving in the mutuality

---

4. Matt 22:37, 39.

of that love. In this writer's opinion, that is what the American ideal is, not an empty freedom to self-define, but a series of beneficial relationships based in the love of God and mutual accountability, uniquely expressed in a moral democracy.

Superior to our right to self-determination, that love is a higher ideal which no individual, or group of individuals (social or political bloc), can alter or influence. It is the ideal from which *all* of our rights originate. Therein our voluntary subordination to each other is not influenced by our personal political or social agendas. While secular law is clearly influenced by those relative agendas, the Law of God, the superior ideal, is not, rendering it the ultimate equalizer.

Subordination to this common ideal requires neither agreement per se nor compulsion. It requires *humility*. Humility requires belief in order, a higher superior truth or power—existing outside of and above one's self, and a willingness to submit to its influence. Humility, like a catalyst, allows us to freely interact with and utilize, but never change, that power. Nor is it used up in the process. Yet the divisive exercise of personal sovereignty and need for approbation—the all-consuming demand that others accept and conform to our self-image—has killed it. In the relative process of defining ourselves, that most rare and valuable of human ideals, humility, has been lost. And lost with it is our fraternity—the cohesive relationships that bind us all together as a society and nation.

Addressing the systemic evil in this nation (or world) corporately through law and policy, therefore, without first addressing it within ourselves individually, is futile. The source of systemic evil is not governments, corporations, movements, or social, religious, or political groups. These entities are merely conduits or tools of individual expression. The source is, and always has been, *the individual* who wields that tool. But our aversion to self-assessment is so strong that we would rather change society altogether just to avoid having to do so—passing on to others our personal accountability.

In our pride few will openly admit, "*I contribute to systemic evil.*" Systemic evil, if it exists at all, is just some vague philosophical concept about which nothing practical can be done. We are unable, or unwilling, to step back and view the larger picture, the single basis for it all: our undue self-interest or sin. Like a disease, sin is systemic—inside each and every one of us. When combined with that of others, it is amplified, globally systemic.[5]

5. In many ways the global COVID-19 pandemic has been an apt metaphor for the

7

Sin. Eyes glaze over at the word as they have for millennia. The skeptic sees sin as a matter of unfair rebuke, an assault on one's personal sovereignty, and immediately sets up barriers. Sin is a nag, a reminder of judgment and consequence, and thus ignored. Better yet is no God, no sin, no good or evil, no judgment, only relative behavior. For the atheist, human nature is what it is—rational and irrational. The best we can do is deal with the issues as they arise. Our civil and criminal judicial systems exist for that very reason. The endless collisions between relative good and bad supply ample fuel for those overtaxed machines.

The Christian believer, however, takes a much broader view of sin, understanding it as the state of not just themselves but *all* creation or nature, and faith, a holistic means of approaching that nature honestly and constructively. That approach acknowledges that the very first, and best, place one addresses systemic evil is within oneself internally (as an integral part of that nature), and not externally in grand political or social gestures, or by otherwise shifting personal accountability.

The way we view individual sin and its effect on personal accountability determines the difference between freedom and slavery, democracy and authoritarianism. The facilitator of that shift is a growing bureaucracy to which we cede our individual power and liberty, ceded to others desiring and able to abuse those tools for their own ends. Conceived in our lack of accountability, this nation's slide into socialism is merely a logical extension of that process.

For the believing Christian the answer to the problem of sin and lack of personal accountability was provided over two thousand years ago in the example of Jesus Christ, in the humility of shared love and personal sacrifice. Those founders who accepted and practiced the Christian ideal no doubt earnestly believed that there was a direct connection between personal accountability and faith, that accountability was primarily a function not of secular duty or receipt of a contractual quid pro quo, but of spiritual love. That spiritual sacrificial love—the higher ideal—would guide the formation and maintenance of all our relationships, even those comprising government. It would give real spiritual substance to the secularized

---

disease that is systemic sin. The virus is systemic and pervasive. It disrupts and can destroy. Like sin, we cannot see it, but its harmful effects are clear. Moreover, the battle over its true origins, and between voluntary and forced compliance with COVID-19 safety measures, ostensibly to control its spread, represents well the larger conflict between the powers of the individual and government—between internal and external control of our sinful nature, which is itself the basis for our current national disunity.

maxim *do unto others as you would have them do unto you* by placing it in the context of God's superior Law.

The secular response to this failure of accountability, or sin, is the requirement of more law and regulation, more governmental intervention to compensate. In our lack of accountability, government, or power, steps in ready and willing to relieve us of the burden of that voluntary self-regulation as an unnecessary complication to a simpler life. But the question remains: who is freer—individuals who, in the absence of secular law, must regulate themselves, or those whose lives are ordered for them by the government and those in power?

This work examines that question from a Christian's perspective, arguing, in part, that Christian salvation, when properly understood and applied, provides the means for regulating oneself that secular law is incapable of supplying, thereby providing greater personal freedom and minimizing the need for that law and, hence, the government required to enforce it. That mechanism is the humility supplied by our willing submission to a higher law or higher truth, sourced in a perfect God; a perfect law by which we measure our secular law and justice. It argues that the loss of that humility is caused by our having separated divinity from morality, thereby relativizing or marginalizing truth, and thus our personal responsibility to others.

Finally, it examines our disunity through the perspective of Christian love and the rational (albeit, for many, uncomfortable) relationship between the Christian faith and America's unique democracy. It considers the effects of our systemic disunity on that democracy and presents a broad comparative overview of basic political theory, law, and faith as they interact and define the relationships comprising government.

1

The National Storm
A Picture of Disunity

ABOUNDING IN THIS OFT-REFERENCED city upon a hill,[1] systemic disunity infuses and erodes our most basic relationships—those foundational relationships comprising family, school, church, and business. And nowhere is that disunity more painfully evident than in government—the seat of secular power. How well, and how soon, we address the source of that disunity may well determine the ultimate fate of this nation and its democracy.

At its core, our collective disunity is a function of our individual pride, an unwillingness to cede some part of ourselves for the sake of

---

1. With inspired foresight the precarious economic, political, and social situation in which we now find ourselves was envisioned at a founding moment of this country—in the remarkable words of John Winthrop who, motivated by the passage in Matthew 5:13–14 as to the purpose of our Christian faith, brilliantly integrated the metaphor of a "city upon a hill" (a reference to Zion and the righteousness of believers) into a sermon entitled "A Model of Christian Charity", delivered to the Puritans aboard the ship *Arabella* just prior to their landing in New England in 1630. It reads in part:

> *For we must consider that we shall be as a city upon a hill. The eyes of all people are upon us. So that if we shall deal falsely with our God in this work we have undertaken, and so cause Him to withdraw His present help from us, we shall be made a story and a by-word through the world.* We shall open the mouths of enemies to speak evil of the ways of God, and all professors for God's sake. We shall shame the faces of many of God's worthy servants, and cause their prayers to be turned into curses upon us till we be consumed out of the good land whither we are going.

Winthrop, "A Model of Christian Charity," 10–11, accessed at http://www.winthropsociety.com/a-model-of-christian-charity (emphasis in original).

those relationships. Our government is paralyzed by partisanship, not of legitimate political or social ideas, but by personal animosity, lack of trust, and self-interest. There is no end of valid ideas for beneficial change, yet nothing changes. Out of self-interest we hide our true motives. Perception must belie reality so that personal advantage and a positive image—our vanity—may be maintained.

The storm of disunity is created in the means of controlling that image, in clouding the truth. Inside the cloud we have become numb to that storm, rendered helpless by its extent and complexity. Its weight keeps us focused on ourselves and on those things we need to survive each day. Mired in the day-to-day struggle, we lose sight of those things that conspire together to feed that disunity—mindless, even, of our own contribution to it. In our distress and confusion, we are manipulated toward shelters of false hope, those seemingly offering the greatest safety but which exact a hidden cost, our ultimate freedom.

Whether merely a symptom of, or prime contributor to, this storm, the proactive news media has found a home at its heart. As supposed guardians of truth, broadcast/electronic and print news outlets nurture that unruly child with near constant hyperbole, revealing the hallmark of senseless, futile debate: deaf partisan extremes. Neutrality in reporting is breathing its last; the line between news and commentary is obscured. In an unprecedented effort to interfere with and influence public opinion and, hence, national policy, media bias fans the flames of our disunity, inciting contempt, vitriol, and even violence.

For the same reasons, popular social media outlets are censoring and/or slanting content, becoming willing propaganda agents endorsing favored social and political ideologies and agendas, censoring out voices with which they do not agree. Yet along with sports and entertainment pro-gramming, even product and service providers and their advertisers feel in-creasingly compelled to link their marketing campaigns with commentary on social justice. While it surely is their right to do so, it has less to do with the welfare of this nation than it does with targeting new demographics, flashing a false badge of righteousness, hypocritically leveraging the trend for purposes of generating power, influence, and, of course, money.

Individuals are being tried, convicted, and ruined in the media by mere accusation and/or political association. Social and political change is being forced at the expense of our constitutional right to free speech, as-sociation, and due process by individuals who either have no idea or, in the pursuit of power, do not care what true democracy is all about. The disdain for individual due process and presumption of innocence is at the core of authoritarian rule, an alarming, and very real, concern.[2] Those things we have taken most for granted are the things most easily lost.

Selective investigations and prosecutions by the Department of Justice and federal law enforcement executives reveal corruption, double standards, and unaccountability—by those whose very job it is to ensure that our laws are evenly enforced. The hard work and integrity of the rank-and-file is severely diminished and morale destroyed by the political operatives leading those agencies. It is hard to imagine a more frightening or demoralizing reality than such corruption within the arm of our democratic government tasked with law and justice. Clearly, "relative" law and justice favor those in power.

Further, members of the judiciary, rather than honoring their oaths to serve as neutral arbiters of existing law, appropriate the function of Congress by legislating from the bench, acting in essence as a *super legislature*, running interference for the party affiliations or personal political ideologies or politicians they support.[3] The public loses trust and faith in true

2. The September 27, 2018, confirmation hearings on President Trump's nominee to the United States Supreme Court, Judge Brett Kavanaugh, provide a worrisome example. The hearings were held hostage by political infighting as a result of Judge Kavanaugh having been subjected to lurid, unsubstantiated eleventh-hour accusations of criminal sexual impropriety, claims that could and should have been investigated long before but seemingly withheld for purposes of timing and effect. Due process lost out to political expedience by placing upon Judge Kavanaugh the burden of establishing his own innocence. Thus, guilt by mere accusation—until later proven innocent. Such a burden, in any venue, runs contrary to due process and equal protection of the laws of this nation, revealing at best complete ignorance of, or at worst the utter contempt many have for, our democracy. The presumption of innocence has been a mainstay of our justice system since this nation's founding. Without it this nation would be no better than so many other lawless, authoritarian regimes that have marred world history.

3. One of the major contentions in the Senate Judicial Committee hearings (October 13–15, 2020) on the appointment of Amy Coney Bennett to the U.S. Supreme Court has been Judge Bennett's insistence on being an "originalist" or "textualist" as to her approach to interpreting the Constitution and laws, as opposed to one who believes in the constant evolution of the Constitution and, hence, its interpretation given changes in the prevailing political/social winds. One of the purposes of the narrower textual interpretation of statutes is to maintain an "independent" judiciary by shielding it from claims of bias or outside political pressure to apply an interpretation of statutory language not originally intended by the legislature at the time of its enactment. Likewise the approach obviates the need to inquire about a judge's personal social or political views in the process of filling judicial vacancies—leaving the focus on the more important inquiries about the judge's qualifications and temperament. The Constitution provides not for the election

justice being served by an honest, independent judiciary whose job is not to create law but simply to interpret and properly apply it.

As for Congress, running for office is a blood sport. The victor's trophy is a seat in a polarized body where ego-driven power politics play out to an acrimonious stalemate. Calls for internal investigations grow, not as legitimate exercises of oversight, but as means of political leverage. Nothing gets done. There is no dialogue. No one is listening. Civility and order are lost. Opportunities are wasted. Money is squandered. The people are being brought to their knees by an imperious government that is spending them into submission, enslaving them to the crushing national debt. Only the politicians and their lobbyists prosper, revealing what they desire most: power and wealth. What is best for the nation and its people is mere afterthought. Citizens feel helpless. The nation suffers at home and abroad from a lack of confidence and respect.

College campuses, once bastions of free speech and exchange of ideas, have instead become zones of political correctness, safe speech, and even violence intended to oppress the free expression of contrary opinion through fear and intimidation. There, young, impressionable students are being told what their social and political priorities should be rather than being given the tools they need to determine those things for themselves. To create an ideologue now, is to assure a future political asset.

That indoctrination begins with parsing the English language for subtle cues demonstrating intentional bias—"micro-aggressions"—provoking offense and anti-cultural hostility. Oversensitivity is cultivated to facilitate a triggered Pavlovian-type response.[4] The students *are* the unwitting lab subjects, experiments in social engineering—indoctrination—designed by a manipulative academia bent on shaming them into believing that if

---

of federal judges, but for their appointment (with bipartisan senate judicial committee examination)—specifically because elections are political exercises that potentially leave candidate judges beholden to the demands of the political party or financial machine supporting the campaign. Most importantly, originalism helps preserve our system of checks and balances by maintaining power in the people—via Congress—to enact laws, and not otherwise ceding that power to a judiciary whose job is not to make law, but rather to interpret and apply it.

4. Dr. Ivan Petrovich Pavlov's famous 1904 experiment involved conditioning a dog to salivate (a physiological response) upon hearing a bell at feeding time. Thereafter the dog would salivate whenever the bell was rung. Hypothetically, what if, instead of a dog, the subject was a student; instead of a bell, a triggering word; instead of salivation/hunger, anger and discontent? See NobelPrize.org, "Ivan Pavlov, Biographical," accessed at https://www.nobelprize.org/prizes/medicine/1904/pavlov/biographical/.

they are not anti-issue activists, they are themselves the issue. Innocence is abused by those in positions of power in the name of higher education. Indeed, simple love of country is hypocritically denounced as fascism or populism, recycled pejoratives among those who see the nation's unique democracy as a stumbling block to the extremes of either anarchy or a one-world order. Hope is lost to fear.

We were all told as eager, fresh-faced youths that we can change the world for the better. But what we were not told is that we have to destroy our past, our history, in order to do it—an unreliable history that has been continuously chronicled by biased historians. Today, rather than learning from it, history is being erased as if to purge us of our institutional sin, to propagate the lie that the new, more enlightened social and political order will never make another mistake.

Who better to indoctrinate our young children with this new reality than those with whom we have entrusted their education? Manipulating a captive, naïve audience is an egregious abuse of that trust. Parents exercising their fundamental constitutional right to redress concerns over that abuse of trust, as well as the local public school board policies at the core thereof, now have the direct attention of the United States Department of Justice and the FBI. Lumped in with the likes of domestic terrorists, those concerned parents now require—according to our government—heightened scrutiny as potential national security risks.[5]

Conjuring up images of history's past totalitarian regimes, such governmental intrusion could not be more unconscionable. The direct interference in local educational/political affairs by the law enforcement arm of the federal government has a severe chilling effect on people's rights to free speech and association[6]—in the act of being responsible parents—

---

5. See Office of the Attorney General, "Partnership among Federal, State, Local, Tribal, And Territorial Law Enforcement," accessed at https://www.justice.gov/ag/page/file/1438986/download. U.S. Attorney General Merrick Garland, who penned the memorandum, was President Obama's unsuccessful 2016 nominee for associate justice to the U.S. Supreme Court.

6. As further evidence of the DOJ's willingness under AG Garland to intrude upon First Amendment speech and association rights (religious), similarly under the huge banner of national security, a January 23, 2023 internal FBI memo entitled "Interest of Racially or Ethnically Motivated Violent Extremists in Radical-Traditionalist Catholic Ideology Almost Certainly Presents New Mitigation Opportunities," citing a Southern Poverty Law Center list of Catholic organizations it considered hate groups, was leaked on the internet on February 8, 2023, purporting, in part, to equate a group advocating the use of Latin in the Catholic Mass with radical, violent right-wing extremists. When

protecting their children from indoctrination and abuse as political and social pawns. From a government that should have *all* of our best interests at heart, it is an action hard to justify. But much like the politicized DOJ and judiciary system mentioned above, without restoring that trust, people will continue to lose faith in an education system comprised of self-interested individuals or groups bent on misusing that platform by intruding into the sanctity of family in order to impress upon our most valuable resource their personal social and political agendas.

Further, the lack of any comprehensive national policy regarding border security and immigration here at home only highlights our deep political and social divisions. The existence of borders now appears to be merely a political matter because, like our new self-image, borders define. We prefer fluidity in the act of defining. Propelled by corruption and economic/political turmoil in their home countries, uncontrolled migration of peoples across national borders necessarily heaps debilitating economic, social, and political stress upon the host nations.

In the short term are the humanitarian issues—the immediate care of those suffering from things often beyond their control. The long term is mired in a futile policy debate between those championing open borders, those tacitly desiring the importation of cheap labor and/or votes, and those striving to maintain secure borders and national sovereignty. Under cover of confusion and inaction, however, crime and drugs flow in. The lack of any concerted effort by government to address the problem suggests only hidden personal agendas—social and/or financial. The political climate is one of entrenched partisan extremes, not of compromise. In the wake of those extremes, sanctuary cities and states have arisen in this country, usurping federal immigration law with a form of local foreign policy, creating more "us versus them" disunity in the process.[7]

---

confronted by the Catholic News Agency, the FBI claimed it would retract the report from its system as not meeting its exacting standards. The FBI memo may be viewed at https://www.catholicnewsagency.com/news/253600/fbi-retracts-leaked-document-orchestrating-investigation-of-catholics. Because of its anti-democratic political and social implications, the mere existence of investigations of this kind evince the current government's authoritarian desire to manipulate, rather than serve, its citizens.

7. For example, California's State immigration legislation, SB-54, was signed into law by Governor Jerry Brown in October 2017, effective January 1, 2018. It codified and extended the concept of sanctuary cities state-wide by prohibiting state and local police from using a person's immigration status as a basis for arrest and limiting law enforcement's discretion to communicate with federal immigration authorities to certain instances where the arrested individual has been convicted of certain serious or violent felonies.

Finally, whether here in this country or any other, regardless of any system of government or justice, the most insidious source of our relational disunity—the broken family structure—ranks perhaps highest of all. Nowhere has self-interest so deeply inflicted more damage to this nation (and world) than the destruction of the primary relationships or bonds between husband and wife and parent and child. In many respects it is the death of love, loyalty, and security, the life-affirming glue of all healthy relationships, and hence society.

A child learns to navigate society from the moral relationships within his or her family. True social justice begins, therefore, in the family—in mutual love, respect, and accountability. A broken community owes its existence to the broken family. When the family fails, the aimless child wanders perilous streets, easy prey for the hordes of influences anxious to take advantage of their naiveté and lack of moral foundation (if not some form of abuse or crime, then surely a manipulative education system). The truth is that not everyone within the community has their best interests at heart. Unable to rely on those relationships, we turn to the government. Now *in loco parentis*, the government (via the public school system) manages the children's futures, without also accepting the equally important parental responsibility, discipline.

We concede the failure of the family by shifting accountability for that failure—the child at risk—onto the community. The growing reliance on risk spreading is a burden the broken community can only partially bear. That is today's reality. Viewing that internal failure as an external "community" problem calls for external governmental solutions. The governmental solution necessarily involves politics, influence, and money, ruled by the same self-interest and lack of accountability at the core of the problem. The buck is passed, but the underlying problem remains: the broken family. The dysfunction is self-perpetuating.

So, the scars of that neglect are carried out into the world, inuring us to the difficult realities of life, hardening the shell, making us ambivalent, insensitive, and untrusting. It has surely contributed greatly to crime and poverty. Isolated and powerless, we live perpetually on guard, waiting for the inevitable disappointment of another failed relationship, of once again being taken advantage of. Without that loyalty and security, the unbearable desire to fill the void can lead us to some very dark places, places of enslavement by resentment, cynicism, and failure.

What does it all say about us? One thing is obvious: we are exceedingly unhappy. Our unhappiness is the fault of others. Others need to change. Rather than finding that happiness within ourselves, we must manipulate others to conform to our will, to our own sense of fairness or justice—to our personal reality. We must change the system and establish control. Only then will we be happy, complete. That is, until someone else more powerful than us comes along and changes it to suit themselves, and we are again unhappy. Then the cycle begins anew—i.e., social reform via survival of the fittest.

On any given day, that is what the unpleasant snapshot looks like. So preoccupied with ourselves and our image are we, that we fail to see the big picture. Everything is manipulated to divide. We thrive on blame. Clearly neither secular law nor policy can fix our self-perpetuating disunity. Unabated, the storm swirling about us intensifies. The simple solution, throwing money at the problem through uncontrolled taxes and spending, only feigns meaningful governmental action, rewarding those who either lobby for, or administer, that money, enslaving all of us to perpetual debt.

Hell, like insanity, is doing exactly the same things over and over again expecting a different result. Try as we will, law and policy may change, but the results, unfortunately, do not. Self-interest always prevails. To his eternal frustration, Garcin, a character in existentialist[8] Jean-Paul Sartre's 1944 play, *No Exit*,[9] ultimately surmised that hell was other people. We are eternally slaves to their judgments, deceits, hypocrisies, lack of respect, and annoying idiosyncrasies—their self-interest—proof that our misery is the fault of others. Our true freedom is impeded simply by the existence of others.

But such vanity illuminates the real issue: self-deception. There is no escaping ourselves. In a Godless world we each contribute to another's hell by ignoring our own. To say, then, that "we are primarily good" is to ignore the great weight of the evidence, the pervasiveness of systemic evil and its need for advantage. Its seed lives in each of us—perverting the good. If it did not, this nation would surely look much different than the one captured in the picture above.

8. The Merriam-Webster Dictionary defines existentialism as "a chiefly 20th century philosophical movement embracing diverse doctrines but centering on analysis of individual existence in an unfathomable universe and the plight of the individual who must assume ultimate responsibility for acts of free will without any certain knowledge of what is right or wrong or good or bad." *Merriam-Webster*, s.v. "existentialism (n.)," https://www.merriam-webster.com/dictionary/existentialism.

9. See Sartre, *No Exit, and Three Other Plays*.

2

The Power of Confusion

ACTIONS REFLECTING OR PROMOTING that disunity reveal a deep contempt for the nation's people who are simply an expendable means to a selfish, political end. We are forced to expend all of our time and energy focusing on the bad, and never the good, as if life were one long knee-jerk reaction. Apart from shutting down all forms of communication, there is no rest from the constant turmoil, no room to breathe. It is the new norm in which we all live. In an instant, that constant discord and pessimism, that staggering irony and hypocrisy in this nation of freedom, is electronically aired worldwide with destabilizing effect, all at the expense of truth and civility. Knowing who to trust or what to believe in the resulting confusion is all but impossible.

But that is the point. Confusion is a useful tool, used to manipulate power and control. Those seeking power know that perception is infinitely more useful than truth. So there is method to this madness. Everything under the sun—every action, every statement, every opinion—is intentionally politicized, spun for advantage, and misused to divide, to destroy faith and confidence in our social and political institutions. Nothing is true or false. There is no objective right or wrong, no good or bad, only *relative* opinion and application. All expression is steeped in social commentary, angst, and dissatisfaction.

Whether in the broadcast media, the houses of government, the ivied halls of academia, or the sanctuaries of radical religion, the goal of such propaganda is the same: *disunity*. Disunity is the perpetual engine of manipulation and change in the constant struggle for power and influence. In the process of leveraging that disunity, the underlying principles of our democracy are intentionally suppressed. Without a solid reference point from which to critically examine that which we are being told, we are more easily swayed. Rather than serving as a secure, unifying system of government—a model of freedom—our democratic republic becomes some odd relic that no longer fits or reflects our changing image or values.

It is reasonable to ask why this is all happening. Some say those with tacit or veiled power, who operate outside the public eye and are not subject to the light of constitutional checks and balances or an unbiased press, are manufacturing a national crisis by purposely manipulating our individual and national identities. Stoking gender confusion, racial animus, and crime; opening borders to change national demographics; and stressing the economy to create dependency upon government intervention and hand-outs, is all about transferring power—not between political parties, but directly from the people to the government and those who actually control it.

Others would say that democracy is already dead—at the hand of corporate America and unchecked capitalism. The late nineteenth-century robber barons who helped thrust us into an age of improved transportation, technology, and communications paved the way for a soulless, self-interested ruling class lobbying, manipulating, and bribing politicians in government to do their bidding—not as a matter of facilitating a better ideology, but of garnering more power. While those improvements did in fact provide opportunities for employment and advancement, the possibility of a better life was merely a shiny object distracting us from the source and motives of real power, a shadowy fascist military-industrial cabal wholly insensitive to an expendable, or replaceable, working class. Ours is a democracy in name only.

Each blames the other for the nation's decline. Despite their differences, there are elements of truth to both. The one thing these positions do share in common, binding them together and explaining our precarious national disunity, is the unmitigated will to misuse others for self-advantage. Apathetic, unknowledgeable citizens make easy targets. But for our human nature, our hatred, vanity, and greed, there would be nothing for those powers grab onto, to use to pit us against each other. Giving in to it, we willingly cede our individual power to the government for the sake of that shiny object. Democracy and freedom die as a result. Authoritarianism is born, quietly growing stronger in our apathy.

For this very reason, unbiased education about our government and our history is imperative. As American citizens, it is our duty know the substance of our democracy, to understand it as compared to other political theories and forms of governments. Rather than manipulate our educational system (and students) for political ends, we must, to the best of our ability, hand that unbiased technical knowledge down to our children so that they have the independent means of determining for themselves where they stand—as is their right—rather than being told by others what to believe. It is the means of preserving an educated free choice and fostering personal accountability. Knowledge, free expression, and accountability are the bane of authoritarianism.

It is likewise our duty to understand the struggles our founders endured in creating this nation and its government, and the sacrifices of the patriots who died defending it. Those efforts prove that despite their human imperfection, their most earnest desire was to create a better life not just for themselves, but for all of us. That history, that Herculean effort, defines the real character of this nation, the true body of our national identity—crystallizing freedom, giving it unequivocal substance and meaning.

Without knowledge of our history, we lose the crucial value of hindsight, condemning ourselves to the same failed policies and strategies over and over again. Furthermore, our ability to step back and see the bigger historical picture, the good and the bad, and its application to our current state of affairs, allows us to better consider our individual role within that history. We are not just idle passengers along for the ride. We were meant to participate, to respond. Like that of our founders and patriots, our *individual response* is the ultimate key to this nation's survival, to unifying its people, and to protecting ourselves against pernicious relativism. At its most basic level, relativism is the fog of competing self-interests—the means of legitimizing immoral conduct and suppression of freedom.

In securing that freedom, this country's founders labored hard to give our government physical and legal structure. They did so quite cognizant, however, of a flaw in our human nature—the potentially harmful compulsion to measure everything as it relates to one's self. Government is, after all, a series of human relationships. Those labors resulted in the hedge of checks and balances in a three-branched government.

The early founders who counted themselves as Christian believers knew that true freedom and equality could never exist in a system devoid of a moral imperative guiding those relationships, sourced not in their imperfect self-interest or in the imperfect laws they made, but rather in the *humility* of their faith. In that humility was found a truth greater than themselves, one informed by their spiritual Judeo-Christian heritage. As a moderating factor in our many relationships, the importance of that moral imperative on the application of both the individual and the national will could not be overstated.

The give and take between imperfect individuals and an imperfect government requires us to logically concede that the administration of our rights can never be a perfect endeavor. The Christian sees that administration first through the lens of their own imperfection. It is a means of inward reflection before outward expression and of controlling the natural inclination to use, or abuse, others for one's own advantage. That abuse will always be a risk of a society in which we are free to express ourselves and our individuality without undue governmental interference. Freedom, however, carries with it a great moral obligation to control ourselves so that our God-given rights are not misused and may thus be preserved, intact, for the benefit of all.

While each of us is granted those rights and all the liberties flowing therefrom, their preservation requires us to view them not simply as they apply to ourselves, but as they apply collectively to this nation. Those interests are not always the same. Just as there are times when government must cede to the interest of the individual, there are times when the individual must cede to the interests of the whole.

The First Amendment to our Constitution guarantees, for example, freedom of speech. But the demands of personal accountability and public safety preclude us from using that freedom to defraud, defame others, or incite panic or violence.[1] Technically, therefore, our individual constitutional rights and liberties apply only to the extent that their application does not detrimentally interfere with the rights and liberties of others.

Democracy, and the government administering it is, therefore, only as good as the individual's willingness to cede some of his or her natural liberty for the sake of the whole, i.e., *personal accountability*. That is the basic nature of our democracy—a freedom and equality shaped, paradoxically, by our voluntary submission and forbearance. It is at this point where

---

1. See generally, *United States v. Stevens*, 559 U.S. 460 (2010).

the individual and society meet; where our human will meets secular control. The purpose of our government is to administer that secular control equally and fairly for all.

That process involves a constant balancing of interests, a balance supposedly codified in law and regulation and meted out in their interpretation and enforcement. It is a control to which we must all submit—despite the reality that those laws are not always evenly enforced. For the Christian, however, the overarching principle of spiritual submission to a perfect God and perfect law, as found in the example of Christ's submission to God and thereby all of us—a lesson in God's Prime Law—provides a deeper dimension to our personal accountability, and the means of our voluntary submission to others and to our secular civil and criminal law.

Today, as indicated above, the fundamental precepts of our democracy—liberty, equality, and justice—are being conflated with *self-identity* as though each one of those ideals is defined strictly by our personal worldview and applied solely as extensions of our self-image. Instead of focusing on our similarities and mutual benefit, those things that unite us in our common humanity and purpose, that conflation divides by emphasizing and manipulating those physical, political, or social issues that distinguish us, such as race, national origin, gender, sexual preference/orientation, wealth, political affiliation, and religion—all bases of identity politics. It is an ego revealed, for example, in the drive to censor uncomfortable speech, to words which may challenge that manipulation or which to the hearer may sound insensitive or even hateful.

FREEDOM OF EXPRESSION/SPEECH AND CENSORSHIP

Yet that is exactly what the freedom of expression/speech and the First Amendment is all about, and always has been, challenging our perceptions—or preconceptions—about ourselves and the world around us.[2] Such censorship can have no place in a free democracy that must tolerate *all* speech, even that which may, by some, be considered vile or highly offensive, short of that which threatens or incites imminent violence or

---

2. See generally, Committee on Freedom of Expression, "Report on Freedom of Expression," accessed at https://provost.uchicago.edu/sites/default/files/documents/reports/FOECommitteeReport.pdf. Although it has both supporters and detractors, this report was said to provide the gold standard of academia's response to issues regarding free speech.

breaches of the peace. The United States Supreme Court has in fact held that since adoption of the Bill of Rights in 1791, sufficient public safety concerns may justify restrictions on individual liberties, including freedom of speech.[3] Such is the case as noted above for inciting others to violence.[4]

The public's safety, however, is measured by the immediacy of the risk to that safety, and not by any potential or speculative offense to the hearer. Inflating all speech contrary to one's self-interest to the level of imminent threat or violence, twists the definition of public safety and mischaracterizes the nature of the threat. An imminent threat is not merely a *possible* or remote threat: it is one intended to produce imminent lawless action.[5]

As a partisan defense tactic, however, the goal is simply to prevent the speaker from potentially influencing others to a view contrary to that of the offended hearer. That is censorship. It is more likely that unilaterally changing the definition of imminent threat simply to conform to the hearer's personal tolerance would only increase the potential for breaching the peace by wrongfully suppressing the speaker's fundamental freedom of thought and expression. Speech is power. Any legitimate right is power. Censorship is a means of quelling that power—of denying the individual's right. It is no mere platitude to state that the suppression of fundamental rights, like speech, is the stuff of revolutions. History confirms it.

3. *Stevens*, 559 U.S. at 468.

4. See, e.g., *Brandenburg v. Ohio*, 395 U.S. 444 (1969), where the Court unanimously struck down as violative of the First and Fourteenth Amendments the Ohio Criminal Syndicalism Statute prohibiting speech that purported to punish individuals who assembled merely to advocate the use of force or lawless action without distinguishing it from speech actively inciting—and likely to produce—imminent lawless action. The difficulty, of course, is in defining or applying the term *imminent*. While concurring with the court's decision, Justice Douglas reviewed the historical inconsistency of the court's application of the so-called "clear and present danger" test to determine imminence, which seemed to focus not simply on the nature of the speech and its intended immediate response but also upon the social and political backdrop of events giving rise to the words. For example, during WWI, the Supreme Court upheld the conviction of an individual for distributing pamphlets critical of the war and the draft because of its potential to cause insubordination and interfere with the conscription of soldiers—important governmental goals of that congressionally declared war. Looking back, Justice Douglas criticized its application in that case and others as an affront to the First Amendment, where the decisive factor was not the immediacy of the elicited response but, in the context of that political backdrop, how powerfully the words were spoken or the strength of the speaker's conviction or belief in them.

5. See *Brandenburg*, 395 U.S. at 447.

We may not shut down debate simply by crying foul, invoking the moniker "hate speech"—by inserting confusion as to the scope of the right. The rub is in defining it. It is a much too relative a term to define because it bends to the varied sensitivities of the hearer. There are just too many factors that distinguish us as individuals. Therefore, bad form or hurt feelings generated by slights to our self-image cannot be the test for determining the scope of our constitutional freedom of speech. Falling prey to that emotion is self-defeating, promoting a society so weak as to be unable to stand up and speak for itself or move forward, one that must constantly hide behind the protection of *more* law and regulation—behind the wall of a growing authoritarianism.

Hate Speech v. True Threats

Labeling speech as "hate" has less to do with labeling the speech than it does with labeling the speaker. It is one thing to debate an idea. It is another thing altogether to attack or demean the individual espousing the idea, which is what we do to short-circuit a debate we have already lost—or at least a deeper examination of the merits of our own position. Its purpose is to cast the speaker as evil perpetrator and the hearer as helpless victim. This is tactical avoidance. One can never address the real issues because they are manipulated, instead, into having to defend their character or unduly measure their speech. That chilling effect on speech—the need to weigh every word prior to speaking for fear of incurring some form of liability—criminal or civil, has constitutional implications.

Outside of any legitimate political or social context in which our words might be expressed, thereby invoking greater First Amendment protections, words that incite, defame, or those considered obscene are generally held to lack social value and are, therefore, unworthy of constitutional protection. Yet even unprotected speech is not completely unprotected. Speech always carries with it an inherent right to be expressed. And that to unnecessarily proscribe or censor that speech creates that chilling effect on that right of expression. As a result, any prohibition on speech entails constitutional analysis and the application of some standard of measurement regarding the speaker's state of mind or intent when speaking them. That analysis always begins from the perspective of the speaker's constitutional right to speak, balanced against the need to protect citizens from unlawful conduct.

For example, such unprotected speech also includes "true threats." True threats are "serious expression[s] conveying that a speaker means to commit an act of unlawful violence."[6] Current law regarding true threats holds that despite what the hearer may hear, whether the words are actionable depends on the speaker's subjective state of mind in speaking them, i.e., whether he or she possessed the appropriate "mens rea" (bad intent) in speaking them. Not only that they subjectively understood the threatening nature of the words, but that they intended the violence attributed to them. As with other forms of unprotected speech like defamation, the U.S. Supreme Court has held that the speaker's intent is measured not solely by how a reasonable person would objectively interpret them, but rather that the speaker understood and spoke the words with a *reckless disregard* for their defamatory or threatening nature.[7] In other words, the speaker was aware "'that others could regard his statements as' threatening violence and 'deliver[ed] them anyway.'"[8]

As such, true threats can incur civil and/or criminal liability. However, what are we to think about the prospect of hate speech that equates a word's meaning or content with violence (as independently defined by the hearer and their own personal sensitivities)? The Supreme Court has been fairly clear on the issue of content or viewpoint discrimination. In a recent decision regarding the use of trademarks as a form of free "viewpoint" expression, the Court found that the disparagement clause of the Lanham Act prohibiting the registration of a trademark that "[c]onsists of or comprises immoral, deceptive, or scandalous matter; or matter which may disparage . . . persons, living or dead, institutions, beliefs, or national

---

6. *Counterman v. Colorado*, 600 U.S. __, __ (2023) (slip op. at 6) (citation omitted). Counterman was convicted under a Colorado statute making it unlawful to "[r]epeatedly . . . make any form of communication with another person" in "a manner that would cause a reasonable person to suffer serious emotional distress and does cause that person . . . to suffer serious emotional distress." Colo. Rev. Stat. §18–13–602(1)(c) (2022). Counterman claimed that his actions could not be considered a "true threat" and that his conviction under the statute violated his First Amendment rights in that it required only that a reasonable person would objectively understand the words as being threatening, and not that he actually had any subjective intent to threaten. In a 7–2 decision, the Supreme Court agreed striking the conviction, holding that application of the statute's objective standard of proof violated Counterman's constitutional rights.

7. *See Counterman*, 600 U.S. at __ (slip op. at 14). That "reckless" standard of proof, "offers 'enough "breathing space" for protected speech,' without sacrificing too many of the benefits of enforcing laws against true threats," *quoting, Elonis v. United States*, 575 U.S. 723, 748 (2015).

8. *Counterman*, 600 U.S. at ____ (slip op. at 11), *quoting, Elonis*, 575 U.S. at 746.

symbols, or bring them into contempt, or disrepute . . ,"[9] violated the First Amendment's Free Speech Clause. Rather than forms of "commercial" or "government" speech, trademarks are a form of "private" speech (i.e., they express an "idea"). In the context of private speech, the Court has "said 'that the public expression of ideas may not be prohibited merely because the ideas are themselves offensive to some of their hearers.'"[10] It has further held that viewpoint "[s]peech that demeans on the basis of race, ethnicity, gender, religion, age, disability, or any other similar ground is hateful; but the proudest boast of our free speech jurisprudence is that we protect the freedom to express 'the thought that we hate.'"[11]

As applied to the concept of "hate speech," then, it would seem those attempting to censor or suppress legitimate content or viewpoints would, given the Supreme Court's rulings, run headlong into the First Amendment. But in light of our current culture's ever–expanding preoccupation with self–image and sensitivity to personal offense, the political pressure to alter legal process (via legislation) to facilitate punishment for that offense grows too. For example, equating hateful speech (that would otherwise be protected under the law set out above regarding content or viewpoint discrimination), with "true threat" (which is generally unprotected), might well advance that abuse of process by changing the nature of the legal examination of the words.

Redefining a word or statement itself as "violence" could arguably transform it to non-protected speech: e.g., equating a seemingly innocuous statement like "green hair is unnatural," which someone might find disparaging, with the threat: "I am coming to harm you." Perhaps knowing a particular individual's or group's personal sensitivity to a word or words, and speaking them nonetheless, might, as to that person or group, suffice for establishing a speaker's liability. The speaker's bad intent could be deemed to be built into the word(s) without need for extrinsic proof—a form of

9. 15 U.S.C. §1052(a), a section of the Trademark Act of 1946 (also known as the Lanham Act).

10. *Matal v. Tam*, 582 U.S. ___, ___ (2017) (slip op. at 22–23), *quoting, Street v. New York*, 394 U.S. 576, 592 (1969). Tam, an Asian-American musician, sought to register his band's name "The Slants" as a registered federal trademark. The registration was denied by the Patent and Trademark office as disparaging those of Asian descent. The Court, however, found that Tam was expressing his constitutionally protected idea or viewpoint in the band's name, and that government had no valid reason to interfere with that expression and, thus, its registration as a federal trademark.

11. *Tam*, 582 U.S. at ___ (slip op. at 25), *quoting, United State v. Schwimmer*, 279 U.S. 644, 655 (1929).

strict liability (liability without the need to prove the speaker's actual state of mind). Or, as with true threats, one might otherwise prove the speaker's bad intent by applying the recklessness standard to show that the words were spoken with a subjective understanding of their violent meaning or of the hearer's sensitivity to them, and that they were conveyed with reckless disregard thereof.[12]

Our democracy survives on our ability to speak freely. Yet for those demanding radical change, the ends always justify the means. Fundamentally altering our traditional understanding and usage of language severely compromises the protection speech receives under our Constitution, allowing for selective prosecutions by individuals or groups who find that speech personally offensive. That freedom, which we has served this nation well for the last 250 years, will continue on in name only—until such time as we are honest enough to admit that it died at the hand of censorship and the abuse of legal process, and that the guiding philosophy supporting those actions, authoritarianism, now reigns in its place.

Unfortunately, that dystopian day when tact would have to be thrust upon us by force of law is arriving, the new "PC" or "woke" culture, born in the failure of personal accountability and in the acceptance of victimization and mediocrity. We may not like the words emanating from someone's mouth, but for the sake of the right, for the sake of not merely preserving but promoting real freedom, people should freely speak or write those words without fear of suppression.

---

12. The difference between the strict liability and recklessness standards relating to speech is well-illustrated in the law of defamation—as applied to private individuals and public figures. For example, defaming a private individual by falsely accusing them of a crime is defamation per se, and the conveyor is "strictly liable" for those words without any showing of bad intent—merely that they were spoken, heard by others, and false. The same accusation as to a public figure, however, may evoke matters of public importance. As a result, liability for such speech can only be established by proving that the words were conveyed intentionally, knowing they were false, or with "reckless disregard" for whether they were true or not. See *New York Times v. Sullivan*, 364 U.S. 254 (1964). We are entitled to protect our private reputations, but we relinquish a good portion of that protection by voluntarily placing ourselves in the public arena—subjecting that reputation to the light of public scrutiny. It is not entirely clear, at this point, if or how the analysis of hate speech will be influenced by the differences between private individuals and public figures. But what is clear is that our current image–obsessed society is unwittingly losing its valuable privacy rights by the constant uploading of lives and images onto social media outlets for use as public journals or self–promotion, thereby voluntarily subjecting those lives to public scrutiny, all for the sake of self and vanity.

While our words may not be suppressed, we must, however, each stand accountable for them and accept the non-violent responses they elicit as a cost of that freedom. Accountability, in the sense of alienating others, has a way of tempering the rash or irresponsible. That is the basis of tact and diplomacy—to persuade and unite. Democracy and debate have always gone hand in glove. Debate is indispensable in a free society. In that vital exchange some people will inevitably walk away, however, just as many did after hearing the words spoken by Jesus Christ and his disciples, words they found offensive or contrary to their personal beliefs or self-interests. Many may walk away from the ideas on government, faith, and morality expressed in this essay. That is okay. That is, and will always be, our right. We have the freedom to walk away because the alternative to that freedom is indoctrination—being forced to listen. Being forced to listen is to be forced to conform, to be told what to say and do.

Little else is as effective in garnering political support as pandering to that self-interest or identity. Our slavery to that vanity, that ego, is our greatest vulnerability. Savvy politicians use that vanity to their advantage. Political correctness is the language of identity politics, the art of pandering to that vanity, of compelling respect by delegitimizing or shutting down contrary opinion. Its goal is to end debate by suppressing and penalizing free speech and ideas by destroying the value of common understanding and therein our history. With no past, there is no foundation upon which to build. With no meaning, there is no objective reality.

All that exists is the tyranny of the moment—the survival of the fittest. Political correctness, therefore, is an end-run around both free debate and our foundational rights, ultimately approved by sympathetic legislators and judges who support an "evolving" Constitution. Like fads that change over time, expressing the relative sentiment of the current culture, governing by whim, it is simply a means of controlling the dialogue in an effort to garner attention, cause confusion, create disunity, and shift power.

Secular government cannot legislate that we love or respect others. It can only proscribe specific conduct. Political correctness attempts to compel that love and respect by force of law. It takes the normal proscription of unlawful acts further by demanding that we punish the state of one's heart and mind. Punishing offensive speech is punishing an extension of that heart and mind—a proscription contrary to the First Amendment, to our right of free thought and expression. It is simply a political weapon to bludgeon compliance. Even if speech is banned, we cannot change the heart from which it is spoken. That is the sole spiritual realm of faith.

The punishment of "words" and "wrong thinking" epitomizes totalitarian rule, like burning books, a means of control and indoctrination through fear.[13] Political correctness is, therefore, a secular, undemocratic substitution for the loss of the morality that faith ultimately provides. It is a mechanical response to a spiritual void. The love and respect that we cannot legislate is in fact the foundation of the Christian God's Prime Spiritual Law: to love him, and to love others as we love ourselves. That is the love that we strive to infuse into our secular law—the perfect into the imperfect.

We can express that perfect love and respect without having to cater to each other's vanities. Pandering obstructs the true realization of our freedom and equality, both in faith and in politics, by exploiting the superiority or priority of self. The preoccupation with self and image ignores that we are *all* inherently imperfect beings and that our imperfection has extensive collateral effect. In terms of faith, the Judeo-Christian concept of sin is in fact based on our imperfection relative to a perfect God, revealed in the perversion of self-interest, or pride—the idolatry of self. Sin interferes with our relationship with the Creator God and, therefore, with one another. Yet despite the freedom and equality with which God has so lovingly endowed us, we choose to remain slaves to our own sin[14] and to the sins of others.

This age-old struggle is manifested in the internal battle between God and godlessness, truth and relativism, and ultimately between freedom and slavery. The cumulative effect of our slavery to sin, nationally, is to suppress and distort the freedom and equality embraced within our Constitution. Our mutual freedom of speech and of association, along with our right to procedural due process and the presumption of innocence, are all being suppressed as inferior to the individual's self-image—to the pursuit of becoming our own gods. Freedom and equality are relegated to elusive symbols, goals to which we can aspire but never reach, because in our sin we keep changing their definitions to suit our self-interest.

As slaves, we are victims. As victims, we are prevented from realizing our potential both as individuals and as a nation. Instead of seeking freedom, we are blindly preoccupied with resentment, retribution, and recompense.

---

13. See page 79, n. 14, below. The same objection to the restraint on free thought that forms the basis for the so-called separation of church and state (requiring, for example, the payment of taxes to support the church) is found, hypocritically, in the progressive ideal of political correctness (as a "required" restraint on free thought and speech).

14. "Very truly I tell you, everyone who sins is a slave to sin." (John 8:34).

Victimization is a place that many call home—a place of comfort and pity. But victimization *is* a form of slavery. We are all victims of something in varying ways and degrees. But to remain in that self-absorbed indignation only precludes us from expressing our love outwardly to others. Telegraphing weakness and indecision, it prevents us from moving forward, shining as a beacon of hope and unity to each other and to the rest of the world.

Positive, effective leadership is not hobbled by victimization or indecision. Rather, its confidence inspires us to become stronger, more perfect versions of ourselves, individually and together as a nation. The real answer to this country's disunity lies, therefore, in our understanding of, and willingness to submit to, the principles of leadership, democracy, *and faith* provided by the extraordinary efforts of our founders, imperfect individuals who saw themselves not as victims, but rather humble servants of a more perfect union. Their service should provide continuous inspiration for us all.

The freedom and equality for which our founders so diligently labored are the cornerstones of *both* our constitutional republic and the Christian faith. The relationship between faith as the source of a guiding morality and a government comprised of relationships beneficially affected thereby cannot be readily dismissed, as some would argue, by the blind application of separation of church and state. That concept is often misunderstood and misapplied as requiring what we commonly hear as freedom *from* religion, not freedom *of* religion.

There is in fact a sublime connection between faith and government, one not to be found in any misguided attempt to create or infer a theocracy. It is that true Christianity gives birth to the one thing secular relativism has labored so hard to destroy: *humility*—a unifying humility based in a superior love, a superior power, and hence a superior law, the Law of God. Both faith and government are influenced by the quality of our relationships with each other. Humility is the one ideal indispensable for constructively addressing our innate imperfection and establishing and maintaining the beneficial relationships comprising our government and, hence, our national unity. As a true catalyst for an effective democracy, humility is the direct foil to our self-serving pride and its suppressing effect on our God-given freedom and equality.

3

A Relative Morality

THE LOSS OF THAT humility and the seeds of our division have arguably been sown by those skeptical of Christ's divinity. To be sure, the founders understood that views about God and faith vary. It certainly did even among their ranks. Even one of our most venerable statesmen, Benjamin Franklin, despite being born to Puritan parents, questioned the divinity of Jesus Christ. Looking ahead to the end of his life, Mr. Franklin wryly observed in a letter to Ezra Stiles, then President of Yale University:

> As to Jesus of Nazareth, my opinion of whom you particularly desire, *I think his system of morals and his religion, as he left them to us, the best the world ever saw or is likely to see; but I apprehend it has received various corrupting changes, and I have, with most of the present dissenters in England, some doubts as to his divinity*; though it is a question I do not dogmatize upon, having never studied it, and think it needless to busy myself with it now, when I expect soon an opportunity of knowing the truth with less trouble.[1]

Influenced by European Enlightenment philosophy and its emphasis on our natural ability to reason, Mr. Franklin, like his revered colleague Thomas Jefferson, one of the main architects of our Constitution,

---

1. Franklin, "Letter to Ezra Stiles," (emphasis added), accessed at https://oll.libertyfund.org/titles/franklin-the-works-of-benjamin-franklin-vol-xii-letters-and-misc-writings-1788–1790-supplement-indexes.

purportedly subscribed not to Christianity but rather to *Deism*. Deism posits, generally, that nature is fully explainable through the application of that reason without any reference to the supernatural, and that while God exists and created all nature, along with mankind and our ability to reason, he provides no substantive, current influence on the application of that reason. Nor is he the ultimate source of our morality. Therein the Deist could safely say that the only evidence of God's nature (and law) is revealed in nature itself, gleaned by external physical observation and experimentation, not by any internal, personal revelation from the Creator directly to the created. Those too unsure about the matter, in any event, could at least find reason to claim that God or God's nature was, at best, unknowable.

Despite labeling himself at one point a "thorough Deist,"[2] Franklin determined over time that while the tenets of Deism seemed right to him, they were not particularly "useful."[3] Franklin was a pragmatist! Good was good because whatever its source, his experience and reason told him that it was beneficial. Bad was not. Though acknowledging the beneficial hand of "providence" in his own life, there appeared to him no real spiritual connection between that providence and the revelation of Christ's deity, which he doubted.

Observing that Christian morality and faith had been corrupted by human influence, Franklin questioned the very thing that for the Christian renders that faith and, hence, its morality incorruptible: *the divinity or deity of Jesus Christ*. It would seem that Christ's divinity had been jettisoned in the struggle for power and influence within the church itself and in the desire for self-autonomy. The faith had thereby been secularized—de-Christianized.[4]

From that secular human perspective, however, Franklin's point is quite understandable. In their unwillingness to submit to God's higher morality, and in the struggle for power and control, which history seems to bear out, it is inevitable that people, out of self-interest, would themselves significantly diminish the value of the faith. Faith simply got in the way. If faith, like every other aspect of life, is subject to the ever-present corruption from within, where was an omnipotent God to answer for the hypocrisy of those who corrupted it?

2. Franklin, *Autobiography*, 38, accessed at https://www.thefederalistpapers.org/wp-content/uploads/2012/12/The-Autobiography-of-Benjamin-Franklin-.pdf.

3. Franklin, *Autobiography*, 38.

4. In today's hypocritical cancel culture, it would be the ironic equivalent of denying Christ his chosen identity—as well as that of his followers. It occurs to this day.

As a result, God has failed to demonstrably show us his power. We have demanded that God prove his power—to "put up or shut up"—establishing that the only thing containing our actions is not the application of his superior wisdom (the internal solution) but the threat of a real-time power to physically interfere with those actions (the external solution). There is no real respect for the law. Avoid it if you can. We respect only the mechanism for its immediate enforcement, the stiff boot of authority. And if at all possible, we would rather be the foot controlling the trajectory of that boot.

How else do we interpret God's silence? Where, then, is any real evidence of the divine? Moreover, God erred in giving us free will, the abuse of which has itself destroyed the faith. The Christian faith has apparently failed to fix enough people to make any measurable difference in the world. Therefore, what is the point of the faith? Like Franklin, we can give an approving nod, as quoted above, to Christ's "system of morals and his religion" and try our best to follow its tenets, which seem generally good. But that is as far as faith goes. The rest is up to us in the application of our reason.[5]

Given the extent of this nation's disunity, it could be argued that the sole application of human reason in the pursuit of a good, moral life has proved woefully insufficient. Reason and wisdom are not the same thing. For the atheist the only truth is fact, that which can be proved empirically. There is no empirical proof of God. Therefore, there is no higher wisdom than that which can be measured by science and data, or by consensus. Truth and wisdom become a battle between those claiming better data. The pursuit of better data is influenced by emotion, self-interest, and money

---

5. One observes in Franklin's letter to Ezra Stiles, the early pressure of that liberalizing (or, depending on one's bias, liberating) philosophy on education, considering that Yale and Harvard were originally created to train individuals for Christian ministry. Franklin, however, founded what would become the University of Pennsylvania for the purpose of sharing scientific discoveries. In August 2021, an atheist/humanist, Greg M. Epstein, author of *Good Without God: What a Billion Nonreligious People Do Believe*, a New York Times bestseller, was unanimously elected president of the Harvard Chaplains, which, according to their current mission statement, is "a professional community of more than forty chaplains, representing many of the world's religious, spiritual, and ethical traditions, who share a collective commitment to serving the spiritual needs of the students, faculty, postdoctoral researchers, and staff of Harvard University." Harvard University, "Harvard Chaplains," accessed at https://chaplains.harvard.edu/about-harvard-chaplains. One might reasonably ask, what are the *spiritual* needs of an atheist? The irony of an atheist/humanist leading an organization of faith-based chaplains seems to support the concept of atheism being the "religion of non-religion."

(funding). These influence the methods created to collect and measure that data, and the conclusions drawn from it.

Because we are human and imperfect, our reason is necessarily subject, or slave, to the pressure of our desires and circumstances—and in the preservation of our self-images, the desire to be right, or the desire to obtain (or even hide) a particular outcome.[6] Reason, thus influenced, is subjective because our surroundings and perceptions differ—be it science or history. Our reason, like everything else, then, is subject to our sin.

Using C.S. Lewis's logic, reason is a good thing. But influenced by that old parasite, evil,[7] it can be a bad (or wrong) thing. Our reason is the motivation for our actions and, as noted above, the thing to which evil necessarily clings. So the same human reason at the core of the Enlightenment movement—that which truly produced some of the most spectacular scientific advances of the age—is the same reason invariably weakened by our sin.

For the believing Christian, Christ's divinity lifts God's wisdom, his morality, above that subjective influence, rendering it an eternal, unchanging truth worthy of being honored and upheld—not a basic guideline subject, like any other secular rule or law, to relative interpretation and application dictated by changing circumstances or attitudes. It cannot be altered by our perception or desires. As such, God's morality or higher law is *not* relative, for it applies to each individual equally. It is not subject to the whims of human reason.

It is Christ's divinity that gives his words the force of law. To peel Christ away from his divinity and God's higher morality, then, is to throw away the very thing that, for a believing Christian, renders that more perfect morality impervious to the influence of fallible human reason or self-interest. As did this writer, we re-order the higher good by placing ourselves, our reason, above it (and above God) by subjecting it to the relative interpretation that suits us best. Removing God as the ultimate moral judge of right and wrong places that judgment back into the hands of the perpetrator of

---

6. A current example of this phenomenon might be our government scientists' reluctance to examine or admit the source of the global Coronavirus outbreak as potentially being the Wuhan Institute of Virology in China, either to placate the Chinese government, or to minimize their own complicity in funding virus research at that institute (a collaboration with a unfriendly communist government), thereby opening them up to professional ridicule, loss of stature or funding, political backlash, and perhaps even liability.

7. See Lewis, *Mere Christianity*, 35.

the wrong—back into that evil parasite. Even our weakest reason should tell us that evil is not particularly interested in judging itself.

This effort to separate Christ from his divinity and, hence, the morality of the faith is the very crux of the anti-Christian movement. The Enlightenment seemingly embraced it as a rational aspect of modern philosophy. Scripture reveals the founder of that movement as none other than Satan himself. We see it played out in the Temptation of Christ,[8] the famous colloquy between Jesus and Satan occurring after Jesus's baptism by John the Baptist in the Jordan River:

> Then Jesus was led by the Spirit into the wilderness to be tempted by the devil. After fasting forty days and forty nights, he was hungry. The tempter came to him and said, "If you are the Son of God, tell these stones to become bread."
>
> Jesus answered, "It is written: 'Man shall not live on bread alone, but on every word that comes from the mouth of God.'"[9]
>
> Then the devil took him to the holy city and had him stand on the highest point of the temple. "If you are the Son of God," he said, "throw yourself down. For it is written:
>
> "'He will command his angels concerning you, and they will lift you up in their hands, so that you will not strike your foot against a stone.'"[10]
>
> Jesus answered him, "It is also written: 'Do not put the Lord your God to the test.'"[11]
>
> Again, the devil took him to a very high mountain and showed him all the kingdoms of the world and their splendor. "All this I will give you," he said, "if you will bow down and worship me."
>
> Jesus said to him, "Away from me, Satan! For it is written: 'Worship the Lord your God, and serve him only.'"[12]
>
> Then the devil left him, and angels came and attended him.[13]

Satan did everything possible to induce Christ to relinquish his divinity—for the purpose of rendering him, and the value of his sacrifice, useless as the future payment for our sins. His three-pronged assault all focused on relativizing God's law in order to tempt Jesus to relinquish his power—his

8. See Matt 4:1–11; Luke 4:1–13.

9. Deut 8:3.

10. Ps 91:11–12.

11. Deut 6:16.

12. Deut 6:13.

13. Matt 4:1–11

divine humility. Appealing to human needs, desires, and ego, Satan believed that Christ would place himself, his image, above that law and above all those whom he was destined to save. In each instance Christ exposed Satan's immoral treachery by succinctly placing it in the context of the true humble Spirit comprising God's perfect Law—a humility to which Satan, in his self-deception, was blind.

Satan attempted a bold attack on the very source of the truth and law, the triune God himself in the form of man, Jesus Christ, at the very outset of his divine mission on earth. Vanquished by Christ's perfect rebuke, Satan failed. Jesus went on to fulfill his grand mission, and the Law of God, by dying for us all on the cross—the one perfect, all-sufficient sacrifice.[14] Now hordes of others all step in against the individual where Satan failed against Christ—manipulating language and law for purposes of self-interest, many with the distinct advantage of having a public platform, or position of authority, to abuse.

But in our own spheres of influence, we are all complicit. In manipulating God's law and severing that heaven-earth connection, we have discarded the divine power in the prime moral law that we 1) love God, and 2) love others as we love ourselves.[15] These are two parts of an indivisible whole that *must* be construed together. We can try to love others as we love ourselves, but without first loving God, our creator, we cannot appropriately love ourselves. If we cannot appropriately love ourselves, we cannot truly love others.

Separating the two leaves a secularized Golden Rule: *do unto others as you would have them do unto you*, rendered completely impotent by the absence of God's higher, uniting love. That is the effect of the loss of God's superior morality on secular human law. Most of us can easily latch onto that aspect of Christian morality calling for mutual love. Reason dictates that the love we have for ourselves should translate to love for others. It is logical. We all want to be loved and respected by others. Hence we give in order to get. A quid pro quo is involved—a tacit bargain or contract.

When we buy something, however, our responsibility to the vendor of that item or service ends when payment is made and the item or service is provided. In the absence of some further agreement or guarantee, the

14. At the time Jesus spoke the beatitudes to the crowds following him, he said, "Do not think that I have come to abolish the Law or the Prophets; I have not come to abolish them but to fulfill them." (Matt 5:17).

15. See Matt 22:37–40.

vendor's responsibility to the buyer likewise ends. Value is determined by the quantity or quality of what we have received in return for that payment. If it does not meet our expectations, we look elsewhere. This dynamic often controls our relationships. Our love is therefore conditional or transactional, dependent upon our circumstances and how we personally benefit from it.

Disunity resides in the space between those unfulfilling transactions, in the search for a better contract, a better love. It is in our nature to manipulate life in order to secure a more advantageous deal. But the divine love that renders Christian morality immune to subjective reason cannot be changed or bargained for. It is free. It cannot be hoarded or manipulated. It can only be accepted and passed on. For the believing Christian, *divine love* is the true power and substance behind the morality of the faith, rendering it a higher or ultimate truth. Our love makes us vulnerable to those who might abuse it. God removes our fear of that vulnerability. By empowering individuals and, hence, their government to consistently rise above petty self-interest and mediocrity, divine love unites us all in a higher purpose.

Our faith in that truth, as applied to our relationships, is found not merely in acknowledging the benefits of that love, but rather in *becoming* that love. Neither a mere attitude nor sentiment, it is the fusion of divine spirit and the physical body. In the absence of that union, hobbled by the limits of our human reason, the faith has, as one might expect, been rendered uninspiring and ineffective.

Even many who might be termed nominal or secular Christians accept the value of Christian morality without truly understanding or embracing the divinity that makes it an intrinsic part of us as creations of God. That relationship may be something they have only sensed from afar. Thus individuals may tend to find inspiration, camaraderie, even justification, simply in the external rituals of the faith—the "liturgy"—its order and high pageantry. Or perhaps they merely wear that faith as a badge of goodness without really accepting its costs.

Applying form over substance, however, often yields false justification. Like any human contrivance, ritual is subject to abuse. We honor the ritual for its own sake—for the sake of "image" or appearances—measuring our own image or appearance (or righteousness) against that of others. Yet outward appearances often mask the true heart within. The unification of spirit and body, as expressed in the Prime Moral Law above, gives substance to the ritual.

Marriage is a good example, which for the Christian is not merely a social or legal contract between two people, but rather a dynamic covenantal, spiritual relationship of love between three parties: husband, wife, *and* God. The presence of God continually nurtures and unifies that relationship, which then flows out and unifies the family. In the same way, the spiritual relationship between Christ and the church is often described as a "marriage." Without God's love, marriage is merely a relative, contractual quid pro quo.

For the believing Christian, then, faith's power is God's divine love working through the individual. Being a Christian is therefore not something they aspire to one day a week, nor is it a ritual or duty demonstrating affinity. It is fundamentally who they are. It is their true identity. It is stamped upon them in the process of Christian sacrifice, forgiveness, and redemption. That seal renders believers truly equal in mutual love, an overarching love that filters their envy, intolerance, and pride. Therein the Christian discovers the unity the founders envisioned for this nation and so desperately needed today. To our detriment, that unity has become imperiled by our utterly blind pursuit of self-image—of defining ourselves and striving to conform the world around us to that image.

The philosophical separation of divinity from morality has contributed to a deep rift, not only in our social relationships such as marriage and family, but one significantly influencing the scope of our constitutional rights to life, liberty, and the pursuit of happiness. Arguably, its greatest influence has been on that most troublesome question of *when* an individual's right to those wonderful things initially accrues—at the inception of one's life as a loving creation of God, or when that life is deemed viable, useful, or even convenient in our relative human reason. The latter reduces birth to a matter of relative quality and not God's superior love—the very source of our inalienable rights. Relativism imbues an inherent comparative bias into that birth, changing the very nature of those rights.

Our universal equality and freedom are now subservient to that bias—another person's choice. We are all enslaved by that demand, by the negation of our inalienable rights. The owner of that choice is master of those rights. Another's relative choice, or whim, is now the gateway through which one enters this world. If we are fortunate enough to have been deemed worthy of that entry by its master, we are all now beholden to that choice—that master. There is, therefore, a spectacular irony and hypocrisy in that demand for choice in perpetuating the inherent bias that historically has, and continues to, foment so much dissention and division in this nation based on sex, class, and race.

No clearer—and consequential—illustration exists of the influence of relative human reason, or bias, on science than here, an alteration based solely on desired outcome. The value of life itself is at the very center of our collective disunity, evidence of that battle between the Law of God and the law of man. To the extent we have wrested life away from God, we have appropriated the morality that goes with it. To control morality is to control life.

In the absence of a higher morality guiding relative free thought, one person's freedom has the potential to enslave another. The founders surely could not have foreseen the ultimate consequences of that philosophical difference as having a hand in current controversies such as the abortion debate[16], our autonomy and self-image, or, more broadly, in our collective disunity. Their focus was clearly on the practical aspects of creating a government, difficult enough to be sure, given all the vital issues they were facing. Yet the same criticisms of faith that existed then, fostered by anger about the hypocrisies of the church[17] and compounded by a secular misunderstanding of the Old Testament,[18] today find expression in a misapplication of the idea of separation of church and state.

16. On June 24, 2022, the United States Supreme Court overturned its 1973 decision (6–3) in *Roe v. Wade*, 410 U.S. 113 (1973), finding that the U.S. Constitution never supported abortion *as a matter of right*, leaving the legality of abortion a matter of individual State law and the morality of the issue to the will of the people. The decision, a triumph for democracy, affected a significant shift of power from the federal government back to the people whom government serves. See *Thomas E. Dobbs et al. v. Jackson Women's Health Organization et al.*, 597 U.S. ___ (2022) (Slip Op. No. 19–1392, June 24, 2022). Needless to say, progressives who view the Constitution as an "evolving" document are dismayed by the decision, as the Justices confirmed their proper traditional role, not as political super legislators or social reformers, but rather neutral interpreters of the law.

17. I.e., the question of how the God of the Old Testament could call for the destruction of people, or more generally, how, in any event, a loving God could permit evil to exist in the world, was echoed in 1794 by essayist Thomas Paine, who penned in great detail the reasons for his belief in Deism and complete disdain for organized religion, biblical Scripture, and Christ's divinity in *The Age of Reason*. See Paine, *The Age of Reason*, accessed at https://www.ushistory.org/paine/reason/.

18. In unbelieving mankind's desire for self-determination, God's omnipotence is a bitter pill. Viewing the God of the Old Testament as barbaric and unfair expresses our secular inability to 1) comprehend the concept of an eternal life, and 2) relinquish control over morality. We view God's actions in terms of our finite existence and relative sense of justice, not his identity as our ultimate eternal judge. In order to truly understand God and the Old Testament, we must first come to terms with our own sin. God's ultimate authority to judge *his* creation can be understood *and accepted* only retrospectively—*after*

The question is, could the government they created, a democratic republic, truly last? Or would our relative human reason supplant our humility in faith as the catalyst for its ultimate demise? Using that reason we could, after all, define creator and creation—thus morality and life—if so desired. What small matter, then, would be freedom, equality, and justice?

---

an individual acknowledges, like Job, his or her own sin (lawlessness) and that justice for that sin requires judgment and punishment, not before. Only then can we truly understand eternal life. God's Old Testament/Covenant command that the Israelites drive out the false idolatry and human sacrifice from the land he promised them (see Numbers 33:55) parallels the New Testament covenantal work of Christ ("I am the way. . ." [John 14:6]), through whom we drive out sinful influences from within ourselves—or live with the eternal consequences of our failure to do so, not only for ourselves individually, but, like the Israelites, systemically for our nation. For those who accepted it, Christ's sacrifice would ultimately unify Jew and Gentile alike—equals before God. See Ephesians 3:5–7. That was a revelation of the New Testament.

4

The Great Paradox

Freedom in Submission

IN DECLARING THE FOUNDERS' intent, the preamble to our Constitution famously provides:

> We the People of the United States, in order to form *a more perfect union*, establish justice, insure domestic Tranquility, provide for the common defense, promote the general Welfare, and secure the blessings of Liberty to ourselves and our Posterity, do ordain and establish this Constitution of the United States.[1]

Nothing is perfect. We have all expressed this sentiment, having observed some fault in ourselves, others, circumstances, even in the decay of nature itself. Regardless, we intuitively believe in some ideal of perfection, and we tend to measure imperfection by that ideal. We can assert with some resolve, for example, that in a perfect world there would be no war, crime, poverty, hunger, sickness, or even death. Yet these desires are measured in the first instance by our own relative sense of that which seems "good"—and not by any certainty as to what truly constitutes perfection. It is merely a vague ideal that we, as imperfect beings, can neither fully comprehend nor define, let alone realize, that is, in the absence of some perfect source other than ourselves.

The use of the phrase "more perfect union" in the preamble above was not some oxymoronic assertion that there are varying degrees of perfection.

1. U.S. Constitution, Preamble (emphasis added).

After all, if something is perfect, nothing more is required. It either is or is not. And it is reasonable to assume that the framers understood that no individual is perfect and therefore a union of imperfect people could likewise never be perfect. That reference to a more perfect union actually refers to a *better* union of the states than originally provided for in the Articles of Confederation ratified by Congress in 1781.

The inadequacies of that document in lacking the means for its effective enforcement, in unifying the several states, and in providing the means for the addition of new ones, urged the formation of a new constitution. As a foundational proposition, however, the phrase acknowledges that a state of perfection exists beyond the limits of human ability or reason, and that the only real impediment to us ever reaching that perfection—a more perfect union—is, in fact, our own imperfection, a basic truth about human nature intrinsic to us all. All we can do is strive to be *more* perfect, or better, than before.

Whatever the framers may have imagined as the perfect union in terms of a man-made government, therefore, could not exist—in this life anyway. Otherwise, they would have endeavored to create it. They must have had their eyes on something else. Surely they did not see their task as creating on earth a substitute for the kingdom of God—a theocracy. After all, that Puritan utopian vision ultimately proved unworkable due to legitimate objections to a government-controlled church and the resulting restriction on free thought and exercise. Since the circumstances under which individuals experienced God's gift of salvation were unique to each individual, it seemingly required nothing by way of state intervention for its fulfillment. God had it covered.

Government, therefore, could never compel God's grace or our acceptance of it. Thus, for purposes of secular government, in a system preserving free thought in each citizen, the *right* to believe—or not—had to take precedence over the belief itself. The belief was protected in the individual's freedom of thought. It would protect individuals of faith and nonbelievers alike, leaving both God and the individual free to do as they would. From the believer's perspective God's perfect will would ultimately be done regardless, an acknowledgment that this imperfect life was only a temporary accommodation. From the atheist's or nonbeliever's perspective, the right not to believe was equally secure.

But for the many Christian believers among the framers who viewed themselves as lawful immigrants and citizens thereof, the kingdom of God already existed in their midst, inside them, ruling over them.[2] The appropriate government, then, would be a neutral tool for the people's use, a companion to the superior government of God within their hearts—the seat of real power. The covenantal relationship between the individual and God, and shared with other believers, could not be directly expressed in the form or structure of democratic government, but rather in the lives of the individuals using the tools of that government. Neither a sovereign head of both state and religion (like the British monarch), nor compulsory state theocracy (like an Islamic State/Republic) was necessary in that the wisdom of a perfect God was already at work in the individual's heart, guiding those relationships.

As a testament to the value of this wisdom, the framers of the Constitution took great care to develop a system of government recognizing and preserving the primacy of God "our Creator." A few years earlier, when drafting our Declaration of Independence, they acknowledged that primacy by declaring as one that his existence was "self-evident"[3]—a foundational truth requiring no other proof, an existence that was not a function of pure reason, but of faith. For those reasoning that the only proof of God was creation itself, like the deist, establishing that necessary precursor, God or Providence, was still a matter of faith. Therefore, that which helped justify this nation's independence from England—faith—served as a keystone for the government it would ultimately construct and the gateway through which all peoples of the world desiring a better life would enter.

The framers agreed that while the power of the secular government is derived from the *consent of the governed*, the purpose of that government was in fact to secure—to protect—our *God-given* rights to life, liberty, and the pursuit of happiness.[4] Those naturally superior rights, as derived from a superior God, could never be abrogated or substantively manipulated by

2. Jesus told the Pharisees (scholars of Jewish law and oral traditions), who asked when the kingdom of God would come, "The coming of the kingdom of God is not something that can be observed, nor will people say, 'Here it is,' or 'there it is,' because the kingdom of God is in your midst." (Luke 17:20–21).

3. The second paragraph of the Declaration of Independence provides: "We hold these truths to be self-evident, that all men are created equal, that they are endowed by their Creator with certain unalienable Rights, that among these are Life, Liberty and the pursuit of Happiness."

4. The Declaration of Independence further states: "That to secure these rights, Governments are instituted among Men, deriving their just powers from the consent of the governed."

individuals or the government they formed. Faith, then, would serve as the ultimate guardian of our fundamental rights.

This acknowledgment is of seminal importance. It was indeed a statement of pure faith, the true realm of which is not the earthly government of man, but the individual's heart—the seat of God's power on earth. It acknowledged that humankind, or life, is comprised not merely of flesh and blood, but of *spirit*. Freedom and equality are desires not of the body, but of that spirit—a spirit expressed not by our biological need to live, eat, or procreate, but rather by how we interact with each other in the pursuit of those needs—in the relationships we create. Faith orders those relationships.

Whereas survival concerns the individual, spirit, as it applies to us, requires a relationship. The most fundamental and intimate relationship is that between the individual and Creator—in the command to "love God." The integration of that unique spirit with the individual provided the people a continuing means for unifying in hope, for bridging differences, and permitting successive generations (our "Posterity") to maximize the nation's attributes and grow in excellence despite our shared disability—sin. For when two people are willing and able, in that spirit, to selflessly direct the inherent love they have for themselves outward to one another—as perfected by God's superior love—nothing is impossible.

That Spirit is the substance and power of God's Prime Law. The infusion of that spiritual relationship into the foundation of this nation, and the secular laws it enacts, provides a means for addressing that disability and finding that unity. It is a means of moving from the unity of one to the unity of many—*e pluribus unum* (out of many, one—be it states *or* individuals). Before even comprehending the nature of an enslaving government, it was essential then that the individual have the means for understanding and acknowledging his or her own enslavement to sin, because the roots of an enslaving government are individuals who are themselves slaves to sin.

For the Christian, that sin may also be defined as the substitution of one's personal truth over that of God's, becoming a truth or law unto oneself, thereby forsaking the unity of the many for the benefit of the one. It is an inherent quality in all of us. Like DNA, we are born with it. Sin is not an act. It is the predisposition or potential to commit the act—a state of being. We merely act in conformance therewith. There are many acts which are sinful. But each requires a basic animus common to them all. Challenging the Christian faith for its proscription of any one particular sin or act is, therefore, utterly meaningless because it ignores the entire state of the individual. Sin has no particular respect for politics, religion, race, color, creed, or sex. Sin manipulates all of these things for its own ends—to divide and conquer.

The Christian is as much a sinner as the Muslim or Jew, and all as much as the atheist or agnostic. Sin is an equal-opportunity attribute, one not limited merely to its effect on the human condition, but pervasively to *all creation*[5] in a fallen universe. Christian Scripture acknowledges that our spiritual transgression has changed the physical universe.[6] Therein we wage war on two fronts: both outside and inside ourselves. How difficult it is to find lasting peace from the war around us when distracted by another being waged inside. In a vicious cycle the latter has created, and continually fuels, the former.

Our ultimate struggle for freedom and equality as a nation, therefore, is found in the internal conflict we each have with our own sin—in our internal, personal disunity. Here lies the conflict between the Christian faith and secular democracy—between church and state—over the true source of ultimate authority—God or man. This is why only an internal solution to our national disunity will do, because our national disunity is but a shared projection of our internal conflict.

For the believing Christian, freedom of religion is not simply a philosophical exploration of those age-old existential questions of "Who am I?"; "What is the meaning of life?"; or "What is my purpose?" It is the means of addressing the conflict between our desire for perfection and the reality of our innate imperfection, a purely internal matter in which government is wholly ill-equipped to interfere. Yet the resolution of that internal conflict has a paramount influence on the external relationships comprising government—indeed all of our relationships, because it is the means by which we break the chains of our slavery to sin.

---

5. After Adam and Eve sinned in the Garden of Eden, God said to Adam, "Cursed is the ground because of you; . . ." (Gen 3:17). The Apostle Paul describes that universal slavery to sin thus: "For the creation waits in eager expectation for the children of God to be revealed . . . *in hope that the creation itself will be liberated from its bondage to decay and brought into the freedom and glory of the children of God.*" (Rom 8:19–21) (Emphasis added).

6. For argument's sake, one might ostensibly find an analogy in the proposition that global warming, *if* real, and created by us, is the result of the sin of our unbridled self-interest—in disregard for God's creation. See, e.g., Isa 24:5–6: "The earth is defiled by its people; they have disobeyed the laws, violated the statutes and broken the everlasting covenant. Therefore, a curse consumes the earth; its people must bear their guilt."

This reference to law, and more specifically the law of God and its influence on our secular law, is the point at which the discussion of the relationship between faith and government really begins. Seeking a more perfect union, our founders deferred to the reality of a power greater than themselves in the acceptance of one fundamental, absolute truth: the self-evidence of a superior God and, hence, a superior Law. It was an act of humility, of individual and collective submission, an acknowledgment of a higher order.

How strange that a free nation would be built on a foundation of submission. Submission is a concept the human creature abhors, an anathema to our never-ending quest for complete freedom. Submission *is* slavery. How can one submit to the law of God—or of man—and still be free to do what one desires? What is our freedom if it rests in the hands of others? How can submission and freedom coexist?

The answer to those questions is the great paradox that is *both* our democracy and the Christian faith. The answer is found in the nature of the submission. One can submit either in fear or in love. But for the Christian, regardless of circumstance, one may humbly submit in love without fear. The Apostle John reasoned that "[t]here is no fear in love. But perfect love drives out fear, because fear has to do with punishment. The one who fears is not made perfect in love."[7] In the forgiveness of our sins, our fear of ultimate punishment is destroyed, allowing us to live this life in love. Thus, in submitting to God's love, one masters their vulnerability, or slavery, to fear. The same relationship of love we share with our Creator, serves as the foundation for our willing submission to each other and, thus, the secular rule of law—the complex formula ordering our daily lives.

To submit in fear is slavery; to submit in love is freedom. Understanding the unique freedom that the citizens of this great nation possess requires us, therefore, to embrace that paradox: that freedom—though something we will fight tirelessly to protect—arises out of submission. Our true strength as a nation lies not in our military or economic might. Nor is it found in the supremacy of our secular law. Rather, it is found in our personal humility and submission, first to a sovereign God and then to one another in the pursuit of a more perfect relationship. In honoring each other, and the perfect love defining those relationships, we honor God—and his Prime Law.

7. 1 John 4:18

This humility is grounded in an acute awareness of our own fallibility. It is submission to an absolute, inviolable truth that resides deeply and permanently in our hearts: that God is sovereign and that there can be no real freedom without the perfect virtue, wisdom, and love he provides. That freedom is based in the forgiveness of our sins and, by extension, our ability to forgive others. This truth reveals the best and worst in us all. It defines and divides, yet its essence is unity. Immune to manipulation or relative interpretation, it applies to each of us equally, without exception or alteration. Upon this truth, this seeming paradox, our nation was built—the immovable foundation that eternally supports and sustains an equal and free people.

For some, this paradox we call freedom is an ideal worth dying for. The willingness to die for something is, without a doubt, a radical expression of submission. Many individuals, those we call patriots, have done just that, making the ultimate sacrifice. Is that expression distinguishable from, say, a radical suicide bomber's willingness to die for a religious or political ideal (and in the process taking the lives of others)? What is the truth for which such an individual willingly dies? Is it unity, freedom, equality, justice, service to others, love? Or is it simply mechanical devotion, a single-minded effort to usher in, at all costs, an earthly theocratic or autocratic rule?

Freedom for the citizens of this great nation is more than an expression of blind nationalism *or* faith. It is much more than a right to do what we want, when or where we want. Our freedom is unique because it is based not solely on political or sociological ideologies, but also upon the truth that it is inspired and supported by a divine, perfect order. It is the humble acknowledgment that the timing of God's perfect kingdom, and our entry into it, is his and his alone. We are merely stewards of this world until that time comes. The interaction of the principles of faith *and* democracy defines that stewardship, as carried out by the consent of a well-informed governed, setting this nation—and the freedom its citizens possess—apart from any other.

Other cultures may find this unique freedom and stewardship difficult to grasp. We can impart our political or economic wisdom and structure to other peoples and nations, but that is only the shell of what this nation truly is. At its heart is an integrity born in that superior order. To a culture that does not share or understand this heritage and its relationship to our freedom, that superficial structure is apt to deteriorate into something unintended, or serve as the means to an end other than the prime model for a lasting institution.[8]

Oftentimes it is not our democracy that we seek to export, but simply our influence for geopolitical advantage. We apply that influence as a one-size-fits-all global secular-humanist democracy, while either misjudging or ignoring the true heart of the people targeted for that influence—as if, by definition, any version of "democracy" means freedom.[9] But freedom in a manipulated, relative democracy is an illusion, a fraud. It is no different than any other political or social ideal corrupted by self-interest and the desire for power and control.

It can be argued that the same thing is happening in this nation. Those in power, having lost sight of the historical relationship between faith and government, attempt to use or abuse the secular democratic process in order to realize undemocratic political goals. The virtue and wisdom supplied by our faith in a self-evident God is rejected or ignored. The more

8. For example, in Egypt demonstrations during the Arab Spring led to the 2011 ouster of President Hosni Mubarak, whose secular government had been in power since 1981. The United States extolled the "democratic" election of Mohammad Morsi, only to see the process used as a means for setting into place a regime that could not truly embrace democracy and that for which it stands. The "one-off" democratic election was used to install an anti-democratic (in this case, Islamic-theocratic) government, which ultimately was undemocratically wrested back by the military. At the time, the election of Morsi was supported by President Barack Obama whose support was criticized by those who saw the election as the installation of rule by the anti-democratic Muslim Brotherhood, Sharia law, and the growth of the Islamic Caliphate. Anti-Morsi demonstrations arose in 2013 when Morsi attempted to consolidate power in himself, which shortly thereafter led to his arrest. On September 16, 2017, Morsi was found guilty of having provided state documents to the government of Qatar and sentenced to twenty-five years in prison. This was on top of a twenty-year sentence he was already serving for having been found guilty of killing protesters in 2012.

9. The failure of the United States' trillion-plus dollar, twenty-year experiment in democratic nation building in Islamic Afghanistan played out in August 2021 as the Biden administration's ill-conceived American troop withdrawal allowed, in a matter of days, the Taliban to reestablish control over that nation's capital without a scintilla of resistance from the Afghani military or government. The lack of Afghani will to counter the terrorist Taliban proves the futility of democracy initiatives in nations with anti-Christian sentiments. An August 18, 2021 Reuters® report quotes Waheedullah Hashimi, a Taliban military commander, opining, "There will be no democratic system at all because it does not have any base in our country. . . . We will not discuss what type of political system should we [sic] apply in Afghanistan because it is clear. It is sharia law and that is it." Gopalakrishnan, "Council may rule Afghanistan," accessed at https://www.reuters.com/world/asia-pacific/exclusive-council-may-rule-afghanistan-taliban-reach-out-soldiers-pilots-senior-2021-28-18/. Extract used by permission of Reuters®.

we, in our self-interest, try to rewrite our national history or redefine or "de-democratize" our democracy—just as we have de-Christianized Christianity—the less resolved we become in maintaining those foundational ideals as cornerstones of our relationships with one another and with other nations. The result is to weaken the fabric of our democracy and imperil our freedom.

Instead, we all tend to define freedom as "freedom from absolutes." We despise absolutes—like those imposed by the Christian God. Our pride hates that which seeks to define us. We wish to be free to define or re-create ourselves, our images. We wish to be kings of our domains. The truth is that we have the freedom to do so, the freedom to "choose"—choices for which we are all held accountable. Those choices determine our true character.

Still, while it is true that individuals are free to choose, it is also admittedly true that the believing Christian is not free to redefine the God who, in giving them life, provides that freedom, freedom that is a product of his virtue and wisdom—his truth. Having submitted to that truth, that one absolute, the Law of God is *not* theirs to rewrite. For the non-believer, this is an unacceptable limitation on choice or self-definition.

5

You Are a King

Rewriting the Law of God

"You are a king, then!" said Pilate. Jesus answered, "You say that I am a king. In fact, the reason I was born and came into the world is *to testify to the truth*. Everyone on the side of truth listens to me." "What is truth?" retorted Pilate.[1]

—JOHN 18:37–38

WHEN JESUS WAS ARRESTED and brought before Pontius Pilate, the Roman governor of Judea, he knew that he would soon die. His comments to Pilate, made all the more compelling as some of the last words of surely the most influential person to ever exist, reiterate perhaps some of the most important spoken by Jesus during his time on earth: that he came to us for the sole and specific purpose of *testifying to the truth*.

Jesus had earlier revealed that truth to his disciples when he said, "*I am* the way and *the truth* and *the life*. No one comes to the Father *except through me*."[2] It was a bold, exclusionary truth few were willing to hear, and serves to this day as the primary reason the Christian faith is rejected, even despised, by nonbelievers. It was a blunt rebuke to the individual's

---

1. (Emphasis added).
2. John 14:6. (Emphasis added).

demand for self-determination—rendering that determination meaning-less before God.

Pilate's response is typical of us all: "What is truth?" Historically, this has been our response to the relative or the unexplainable, and certainly to God—to his existence or authority. It has been the response to anything that challenges our personal sovereignty. On a substantive level, Pilate was being handed an absolute that, in his pride, he would not accept. To him, in his relative world, truth was whatever he said it was. After all, he was the governor, answering only to Rome. In that regard, Pilate did, however, un-derstand power and influence. The concept of truth was merely a means to that end—a political tool—something to be manipulated in order to affect a particular outcome. Pilate needed a lie to be the truth. Because he held power, no one could do anything about it.

By means of its relative application, Pilate purposely marginalized responsibility for his actions (both individually and officially) by painting what he knew to be wrong with the brush of governmental authority. He refused personal accountability. And indeed, as the story goes, Pilate liter-ally washed his hands of the matter, thereby clearing the Via Dolorosa for Christ's crucifixion.[3] To Pilate, there was no absolute truth. But Jesus had already preempted that response by informing him that, as quoted above, "everyone on the side of truth listens to me," knowing that Pilate, out of self-ish political expedience, would not. Nor did the mob desiring Jesus's death.

Pilate was aware that those who were handing Jesus over to him de-sired his execution, according to their law, for claiming to be the Son of God.[4] Yet due to the Roman occupation, that law could not be carried out without Pilate's order. On hearing this, Pilate inquired of the prisoner:

> "Where do you come from?" he asked Jesus, but Jesus gave him no answer.
>
> "Do you refuse to speak to me?" Pilate said. "Don't you real-ize I have power either to free you or to crucify you?'

3. "When Pilate saw that he was getting nowhere, but that instead an uproar was starting, he took water and washed his hands in front of the crowd. 'I am innocent of this man's blood,' he said. 'It is your responsibility!'" (Matt 27:24).

4. Earlier that winter, during Hanukkah, Jesus was speaking to the Jews gathered at the Temple in Jerusalem. He was asked, "How long will you keep us in suspense? If you are the Messiah, tell us plainly." He answered, "I did tell you, but you do not believe. . . . I and the Father are one. . . . Why then do you accuse me of blasphemy because I said, 'I am God's Son'?" (John 10:24–25, 30, 36).

Jesus answered, "You would have no power over me if it were not given to you from above. Therefore the one who handed me over to you is guilty of a greater sin."

From then on, Pilate tried to set Jesus free, but the Jewish leaders kept shouting, "If you let this man go, you are no friend of Caesar. Anyone who claims to be a king opposes Caesar."[5]

The leaders, seeking to destroy Jesus, attempted to justify their demands by hypocritically invoking Roman law—which they despised. Jesus did not deny their claims, but Pilate did not see this as a capital offense. He did, however, see it as a political matter that at the time required appeasing those desiring Jesus's death, lest Rome chastise him for failing to maintain control. It was Passover, and Jerusalem was crowded with celebrants. A riot was the last thing Pilate needed. One life was easily expendable for the relative peace or greater good.

Scripture makes clear, however, that the worldly concerns of those leaders for their own social, political, and financial interests, rather than religious ideology, provided the real motivation for their persecution of Christ. Therein we can understand Jesus's statement to Pilate that their sin (their hypocrisy as religious leaders and breach of their higher duty to God[6]) was worse than Pilate's who was ostensibly acting under color of his official secular duty to Rome and those he ruled, a position he owed, like all authorities, to divine providence.[7] Yet in that same self-interest, we all create our own truth. By doing so, we have, both individually and collectively as a nation, separated ourselves from God and God's Law.[8]

Within Jesus's remarkable statement about truth, we see the root clash between faith and government: the government of God (the truth) is continually usurped by the individual's self-interest, and the government of self-interest is continually undermining the individual's faith—the negative pushback to speaking truth to power. Jesus confirmed to Pilate that he was, in fact, addressing a king. Just prior to the above quote, Pilate asked Jesus if he was king of the Jews. Jesus responded by stating, "My kingdom is not

5. John 19:9–12.

6. In particular, the actions of Caiaphas, the Sanhedrin's high priest, who ordered Jesus to be turned over to Pilate.

7. See Col 1:15–16: "The Son is the image of the invisible God, the firstborn over all creation. For in him all things were created: things in heaven and on earth, visible and invisible, *whether thrones or powers or rulers or authorities; all things have been created through him and for him.*" (Emphasis added).

8. Separating morality from divinity in the process, as discussed earlier.

of this world. If it were, my servants would fight to prevent my arrest by the Jewish leaders. But now my kingdom is from another place."[9]

Describing the nature of his kingdom, Jesus instructed Pilate, and all of us, as to the source of his sovereignty: the truth, and that like him, ultimate truth was not a product of this corrupt world. *Truth was from another place.* Pilate, like the group clamoring for Jesus's death, expressed his unwillingness to consider this king's sovereignty because it ran counter to his self-interest which, in turn, revealed his pride. The Romans were pantheistic, having many gods, and standing before Pilate was no god, just a man over whom he had the power of life and death—the ultimate tool of coercion and control. Most of us can sympathize with Pilate's resentment at being told what the truth is. Just as Pilate was king over his domain, we too are kings over ours. And we resent encroachments upon our sovereignty.

In exercising that sovereignty we kill truth—just as Pilate killed Jesus—killed out of expedience. Power corrupts. Jesus established, however, that it is not the concept of raw power, control, or mere consensus that provides the government with legitimate authority to rule. Rather, the ultimate authority to rule is found in the sovereignty of truth, which informs and guides the application and limits of power. Like each of us, government and secular law had to be subject to a higher truth—a truth not of this fallen, corrupt world. God became man in Jesus Christ to, in part, restore that truth, the love of God, into the law of man.

Those founders of this nation who counted themselves as Christian believers undoubtedly understood that power absent that higher truth— the authority and wisdom of God's Prime Law—is vulnerable, like Pilate's Rome, to human corruption and tyranny.[10] Because the impartial wisdom and virtue of that truth is available to each one of us in God's perfect Law, the power derived from it dwells within the people as God dwells among them in the Spirit. It was not to be found exclusively within a king by divine

---

9. John 18:36.

10. Tyranny is an expression of institutionalized sin—in government or faith—where ideological, political, or religious "heresies" are subdued by authoritarian rule. Compare the tyranny of Mao's communist or Hitler's and Mussolini's national socialist dictatorships with the tyranny of *radical* Islamic or Christian fundamentalism. An example of that tyranny expressed institutionally within Christianity is the Inquisition, a Catholic tribunal originally organized in France in the twelfth century, which then spread to Spain and all of Europe in the few hundred years that followed before its demise. Tasked with rooting out heretics, its methods of coercing confession, and subsequent judgments, were carried out with infamous brutality.

right,[11] or even that group of individuals elected or appointed to administer the people's affairs.

Truth, therefore, is real power. The seat of that power is the Spirit of God residing in each individual's heart, exercised collectively for the greater good. Therein we more clearly understand the real strength in the maxim "government *of the people, by the people, for the people.*"[12] Power resides in the people. It is the people who bestow *their* power on the government, a power each of them equally receives from a perfect God. The truth, as presented to Pilate—and all of us—by Jesus, however, was in effect that so long as the people refuse to deal with their innate propensity to sin, thereby accepting personal accountability for their actions (the internal solution), governments will always be full of leaders like Pilate and those desiring Jesus's death, abusing the power given to them, weakly succumbing to self-interest, and imposing that petty, corrupted interest on others (the external solution). We see it plainly in our government today.

Regardless of any disappointment or despair we might experience today over leaders like them, however, the special events related in this section of Scripture establish that, despite our intentions, God's ultimate truth will be accomplished—as it was through Pilate. God used Pilate's self-interest or "evil" for the "good" of his own plan, just as he used Satan for the purpose of revealing his infinite nature to Job (and this writer). Christ's crucifixion would not have occurred when and how it did without Pilate—the timely death and sacrifice God ordained for the salvation of many. That sacrificial death is the prime example of the inexorable force of God's truth. Unalterable by any human hand, our collective hope rests easy in that inevitability.

The struggle for worldly power, however, is, and has always been, a battle not over truth per se, which cannot be altered, but hypocritically over the *appearance* of that truth and, hence, image and respectability. The lengths to which individuals will go in redefining words and language, hence truth, in order to gain and/or maintain power, influence policy, or

11. The belief that the king received his power exclusively from God, i.e., the "divine right of kings", was vigorously refuted by Samuel Rutherford, a Scottish Presbyterian cleric who, in 1644, published his influential work, *Lex, Rex* (*the Law is King*), positing that while God chooses the king, the king's power is derived from the approval of the people he rules as individual recipients of God's Spirit and law (the natural law). Rutherford's views changed the very nature of government accountability, as well as views on the power of the church as it related to secular government. Power in the individual, and the freedom from imperious, unaccountable rule, wove its way into Enlightenment thought, and into our nation's early democracy.

12. Lincoln, "The Gettysburg Address." (Emphasis added).

avoid accountability, attests to the validity of this concept. The constant need to manipulate truth in order to promote our self-interest or desired image reveals the real state of the human heart. As with Pilate and the mob, the manipulation (or death) of truth is the mark of human hands on God's superior Law.

Employing the same insidious technique Satan used against Jesus during his temptation in the wilderness,[13] the first instance of such "manipulation" or rewriting the Law of God, occurred when the serpent tempted Eve in the Garden of Eden:

> He said to the woman, "Did God really say, 'You must not eat from any tree in the garden'?"
>
> The woman said to the serpent, "We may eat fruit from the trees in the garden, but God did say, 'You must not eat fruit from the tree that is in the middle of the garden, and you must not touch it, or you will die.'"
>
> "You will not certainly die," the serpent said to the woman. "For God knows that when you eat from it your eyes will be opened, and you will be like God, knowing good and evil."
>
> When the woman saw that the fruit of the tree was good for food and pleasing to the eye, and also desirable for gaining wisdom, she took some and ate it. She also gave some to her husband, who was with her, and he ate it. Then the eyes of both of them were opened, and they realized they were naked; so they sewed fig leaves together and made coverings for themselves.[14]

The Book of Genesis offers here what purports to be the world's first law proscribing specific conduct of any kind: God's admonition that Adam and Eve not eat fruit from the Tree of the Knowledge of Good and Evil. According to Scripture, the penalty for sin is death—manifested in this life by physical death and in the afterlife by total separation from God and his love (spiritual death/hell).[15]

13. See chapter 3.

14. Gen 3:1–7.

15. The eternal anguish of judgment and hell was communicated by God to the Apostle John as related in the Bible's final chapter:

> He who was seated on the throne said, "I am making everything new!" Then he said, "Write this down, for these words are trustworthy and true."
>
> He said to me: "It is done. I am the Alpha and the Omega, the Beginning and the End. To the thirsty I will give water without cost from the spring of the water of life. Those who are victorious will inherit all this, and I will be their God and they will be my children. But the cowardly, the unbelieving, the vile, the

The purpose of the law was twofold: first, to establish the preeminence of God's sovereignty—the source and power of the law; and second, to establish the existence of sin and its penalty. For "where there is no law there is no transgression [sin]."[16] The law casts light on and defines the wrongful act that it proscribes. God's Law *is* God's truth. We break God's Law and alter his truth by manipulating it to appear as though it means something other than what he intended it to mean; i.e., we embrace the form or appearance of truth over its substance.

In that particular sense one might say that the first sin in Eden was not Eve's eating the fruit, nor Adam's failure to prevent it, but Satan's in spinning God's law in order to undermine God's sovereignty—his truth—thereby manipulating another to sin. It was the condition precedent to their sinful act. It had malicious intent—directed at God—at the expense of Adam and Eve (and, hence, all mankind). In Satan's war with God, Adam and Eve were expendable—as are we all. Still, he did not compel them to eat the fruit and break the law. They did so of their own free will, which he manipulated to his own advantage. He used their self–love, their vanity/image, against them—separating their love of self, from the primary, defining love of God.

The damage was done. Their will was now tainted by Satan's corrupting influence: the desire to relativize and, thus, undermine God's truth for the sake of personal interest. Giving in to that temptation, Adam and Eve lost the ultimate perfect freedom they enjoyed in Eden, enslaving themselves to the law they disobeyed and the punishment they invited for having done so—life in a fallen world. That was their consequence—the force of law. It is ours too, as heirs of their corrupted will and lack of personal accountability.

The spin Satan placed on God's Law/Truth was that God did not really mean what he said when instructing them not to eat the fruit. Therefore, God was not trustworthy—not the ultimate sovereign authority. His law was flawed and therefore not worthy of being obeyed. God was not perfect. Nor was his Law. The implication is that we are, in the exercise of our free will, our own authority, our own kings, and needn't look any further than ourselves to justify our actions. The power is ours to abuse.

Moreover, Satan disparaged God and his truth by insinuating that God was selfish in not sharing with Adam and Eve something beneficial,

---

murderers, the sexually immoral, those who practice magic arts, the idolaters and all liars—they will be consigned to the fiery lake of burning sulfur. This is the second death." (Rev 21:5–8)

16. Rom 4:15.

that he wanted it all for himself. In effect, God was denying them personal advantage. God did not really care about them. Here Satan set up a perpetual conflict between them and God by stoking envy and disappointment in their hearts.

Satan played to their vanity by assuring them that in knowing, they too would be like God. The original temptation was to abuse, and thus corrupt, our free will in order to promote our self-interest or ego—to decide for ourselves what is good and evil—placing ourselves, and our secular law, above the Law of God. This corruption defines the state of all creation to this day. By equating us with God, Satan sowed the seeds of relativism as a diversion to an absolute truth. Relativism breeds doubt. Doubt creates confusion. Confusion generates fear. And fear is the catalyst for manipulation and division.[17]

Finally, Satan placed a wedge of self-interest between husband and wife, causing them to compare the good and evil in each other. The same self-interest separating Adam and Eve from their God now destroyed the unity and strength of their relationship with each other (interfering with what would later be revealed as the Prime Law). As a result, they clothed themselves to hide their immorality and weakness—a new, false identity.

The new enmity and distrust between them would flow out to and infect the unity of the resulting family—the basic building block of society, an infection clearly revealed today in the destruction of the traditional family and ensuing societal dysfunction. It has spread throughout the millennia in the infamous words of Cain, first son of Adam and Eve, who, when foolishly lying to God about having killed his younger brother, Abel, exclaimed, "Am I my brother's keeper?"[18]

As it was for jealous, self-interested Cain, this manipulation of truth is the inevitable result of the desire to be free from authority and the guilt of immorality. It is reflected in a dogmatically secular, relative worldview—and our conspicuous desire to reacquire those natural freedoms we voluntarily relinquished as the compromise for living, and being accountable to each other, in a civilized society. That relativism serves as the clothes we wear to hide the shame of our immorality. It is the means by which we manipulate truth in order to preserve our good image, self-interest, and advantage given our weakened state—our internal disunity.

---

17. This is the primary fear that Christ's superior sacrificial love conquered.
18. Gen 4:9.

But in rejecting the absolute truth to which Jesus testified, the secularist or atheist rejects one of the most basic foundational principles of our unique democracy, the self-evidence and supremacy of our Creator God. With no God, there is no sin, no higher morality; only differences of opinion—or relative consensus. He or she is content to exist within that relative order supplied, as discussed below, by the *social contract* simply because there can be no higher authority than ourselves, limited only by the physical laws to which we are all subject—and the need for personal security (survival).

6

The Social Contract

IN HIS 1762 WORK, *The Social Contract: Or Principles of Political Right*, Jean-Jacques Rousseau, the French political philosopher, reasoned that we are born free, i.e., our *natural* freedom, but that the needs of people's coexistence transform that freedom into something else: *civil* freedom. The social contract can be stated thus:

> "*Each of us puts his person and all his power in common under the supreme direction of the general will, and, in our corporate capacity we receive each member as an indivisible part of the whole* [emphasis in original]."
>
> At once, in place of the individual personality of each contracting party, *this act of association creates a moral and collective body* [emphasis added], composed of as many members as the assembly contains votes, and receiving from this act its unity, its common identity, its life and its will.[1]

This "contractual" transaction provides a logical, reasoned structure to the basic concepts of democracy and freedom. Freedom is of two types: natural and civil. Natural freedom is that to which we are all entitled by virtue of our mere existence as creations of God, i.e., the basis of "natural law," to all that we can do or acquire. And civil freedom is that compromised freedom

---

1. Rousseau, *The Social Contract*, Book 1, Sec. 6, accessed at, https://resources.saylor.org/wwwresources/archived/site/wp-content/uploads/2012/09/POLSC2013.21.pdf.

we retain by voluntarily relinquishing some of our natural freedom for the benefit of the society in which we live, i.e., the basis of "civil law." Natural freedom applies to the individual; civil freedom applies to the group in which the individual is a part.

Notably, any Christian reading Rousseau's words above would recognize them as indeed closely resembling the structure of the "church" itself, *a moral and collective body*—the body of Christ—with one significant exception: that which constitutes the "supreme direction of the general will." As revealed, for example, in the colloquy between Pilate and Jesus above, the secularist limits examination of the supreme direction solely to "human consensus" (in that case, the corruptible, relative will of the mob desiring Christ's death), whereas the Christian first weighs that human will or consensus against God's superior truth (the ideal for which Christ died at the hands of Pilate, Caiaphas, and the mob).

For Rousseau, as cited above, morality arose out of our mutual obligation to control our actions for the sake of the whole, assuming "a moral and collective body." Therein natural instinct is tempered with human *reason*. Secular morality arises, therefore, out of our collective reason, a compromised morality upon which we all (or most of us) have agreed, lived out subject to the myriad laws and regulations we corporately create to assure compliance. In a purely secular democracy, then, morality is defined within the relative power of consensus as expressed in the majority and, thence, in law and regulation.

Along with other European philosophers of that era—such as Thomas Hobbes and John Locke (also proponents of the social contract)—Rousseau's understanding of the role of reason in our interactions as applied to government was reflected in the seventeenth- and eighteenth-century intellectual movement known as the Age of Reason or Enlightenment, which clearly influenced some of our founders like Thomas Jefferson and, as discussed above, Benjamin Franklin.

Having its culmination in the French Revolution (1789–1799), the Enlightenment provided concepts in natural law and democracy utilized in fashioning this nation's Constitution. The movement grew out of the refutation of the divine right of kings, the emergence of new, independent scientific discoveries, and a distrust of an imperious church whose influence in both politics and science was viewed as pervasive and stifling. Yet brilliant scientific revelations of that age, such as Newtonian physics/mathematics, for example, provided elegant, reproducible equations explaining observations in natural law that required no stamp of church approval to establish their inherent truth. The science itself was irrefutable—a peek into God's secret universe.

At the time, those scientific observations influenced the discourse among Enlightenment philosophers like Rousseau about the relationship between God and our ability to independently explain the world around us without reference to matters of faith or the supernatural. They viewed the parochial church—the supposed final arbiter of truth—as inhibiting the unlimited potential of human reason and knowledge.[2] Science clearly provided a means of countering that influence, even going so far as to lead some to question the existence of, or need for, God.

As with Franklin and Jefferson, Deism was one response—that divine or intelligent design seemed a logical compromise. But it is in this estrangement between the individual and an absent God, that one understands the root desire for separation of church and state—in the secularization of morality.[3] As discussed above, it is a notion that misconstrues the intent of the concept as requiring a curb on the influence of faith and religion upon the government when historically the intent was the opposite: to counter the influence of government-sponsored religion upon free thought and religious exercise.

Thomas Jefferson was in fact a proponent of religious free exercise. Referencing the First Amendment's Establishment Clause ratified eleven years earlier in 1791, he expressed the idea of a "wall of separation between church and state" in an 1802 letter to the Danbury Baptist Association of Connecticut, which was concerned about government interference with the people's rights of conscience. Jefferson assured them "that the legitimate powers of government reach actions only, [and] not opinions."[4] The purpose of that wall was to "restore to man all his natural rights,"[5] not power to the government.

---

2. Here again, one might reasonably inquire whether the dissatisfaction in the minds of those philosophers was not so much in the real tenets of the faith (for those who believed), but rather with the inevitable hypocrisies of the individuals and bureaucracies administering that faith.

3. It follows that same loss of morality is evident in the estrangement between an absent parent and child—in the loss of a guiding authority and the resulting breakdown of the family.

4. Jefferson, "Jefferson's Letter," accessed at https://www.loc.gov/loc/lcib/9806/dan-pre.html.

5. Jefferson, "Jefferson's Letter."

He, along with contemporaries such as James Madison (principal drafter of the Bill of Rights), saw separation of church and state not as a means of countering the church's influence on government, but rather the government's influence on the church and the individual's freedom of thought. These concerns earlier arose when, for example, certain states, officially supporting mainstream Protestant churches (some still owing fealty to the Church of England), persecuted itinerant preachers and new splinter churches that were pressing the limits of their desire for true freedom of thought and religious independence.[6]

The secularization of morality has consequences. In 1883, a mere eighty years after Jefferson's letter to the Danbury Baptists distinguishing "actions" and "opinions," German philosopher Friedrich Nietzsche, crediting the ultimate effect of Enlightenment sentiment on those opinions, would indeed declare that God is dead! Objective truth did not exist. God was no longer needed as man had evolved beyond good and evil. He was free of moral constraint—master of his own domain, where nothing but "self" mattered—the new "Übermensch" or superman.[7]

The same year as Nietzsche's bold proclamation, Charles Darwin's cousin, Francis Galton, introduced a pernicious social theory called eugenics (a corollary to Darwin's 1859 treatise, *On the Origination of Species*, and his world-altering theory of natural selection), examining the perpetuation of desirable human genetic traits through *selective breeding* and, by extension, the prevention/destruction of those lives with traits deemed less desirable, e.g., disabilities, mental illness—even race. Galton advanced his theory of eugenics (derived from the Greek term for "good stock") and selective breeding in his 1883 work *Inquiries into Human Faculty and its Development*. In a subsection entitled "Selection and Race," he posed a scientific rationale for racism: "The most merciful form of what I ventured to call 'eugenics' would consist in watching for the indications of superior strains or races, and in so favoring them that their progeny shall outnumber and gradually replace that of the old one."[8]

Not everyone is so merciful. A mere decade after Galton's death in 1911, eugenics received a helping hand from Margaret Sanger, founder of

6. For a well-researched, comprehensive treatment of the subject generally, see Kidd, *God of Liberty—A Religious History of the American Revolution*.

7. See Nietzsche, *Thus Spoke Zarathustra*.

8. Galton, *Inquiries into Human Faculty and Its Development*, 307, accessed at https://cors.archive.org/details/inquiriesintohumoogalt/mode/1up?view=theater

Planned Parenthood in the 1920s. Lending historical/philosophical support for the utility of involuntary sterilizations, abortion, and euthanasia (meaning "good death"), one of her 1930s initiatives was to establish abortion clinics in poor black neighborhoods to affect population control within that demographic—her answer to poverty and overcrowding.

Given the impossible task of justifying Sanger's supposedly noble view on birth control with her apparent racist views on abortion as a means of selective breeding and population control, Planned Parenthood publicly divested itself of its founder a hundred years later in 2020 in an attempt to spin its racist history and repackage its brand as a benevolent and just reproductive health provider.[9] It was an easy divestment—a cost of doing business—of assuaging vital sources of funding, including the government in order to survive.

The goal was to divorce the service they provided, abortion, from what some supporters say was its undeserved racist history (i.e., that Sanger was misunderstood). It is not as simple as it sounds. Abortion on demand, for any reason, at any time, is, by its very definition, a means of selection. The right to *choose* is synonymous with the right to *select*. There is always a preference or bias in that choice or selection. Choice cannot be divorced from its underlying bias. Sanger's bias, like Lewis's evil parasite, lives on in that choice or selection. Thus, just as one cannot really separate morality from God's perfect Law, one cannot separate immorality from that imperfect choice. That is the nature of sin. The motivation may not always be race, but the taking of life requires some form of bias or preference running counter to the higher interests of that life—regardless of any claim of relative social good or sexual equity.

Now with God's demise and Nietzsche's Übermensch, Galton's eugenics also found practical application in Adolf Hitler's fascist, anti-Semitic *kampf* (struggle) for a genetically pure (or perfect) Aryan master race. Perfection was a function of physical attribute and of indoctrination, not the spiritual infusion of God's superior love. The world found itself at war. Millions died.

Apart from those lost in WWII, in the fifty-six years between 1924 and 1980, millions more died by execution, famine, and neglect at the hands of Joseph Stalin, Mao Zedong, and their successors under communism, a

9. See Planned Parenthood, "Planned Parenthood Announces Intent," accessed at https://www.plannedparenthood.org/planned-parenthood-greater-new-york/about/news/planned-parenthood-of-greater-new-york-announces-intent-to-remove-margaret-sangers-name-from-nyc-health-center.

socio-economic plan demanding the suppression of the God-given will to be free—all for the ideal of forced equity.

This very day, Stalin's descendent successor in interest, Vladimir Putin, is invading the Ukraine, killing innocent people seemingly out of a maniacal dream of re-establishing a glorious communist USSR, enlarging influence and the buffer between him and the free world. Sensing a new possibility of leveraging global instability and lack of will from the West, China's Xi Jinping surely eyes Taiwan.

These leaders and their political and economic backers are at the pinnacle of a Godless, relative ideology. The death of God and the triumph of relative, unrestrained human reason enabled their plans—a reason built on the same elitist, intellectual disdain giving rise to Galton's eugenics, Hitler's Thousand-Year Reich, and Lenin's and Mao's communist revolutions, all proclaiming the betterment of mankind. It is the very same authoritarian ideal that today gnaws away at this nation's democracy from the inside, where science, religion, and politics, are all manipulated in the greater struggle for supremacy.

Man was his own god. Individuals demanding secular free thought were now no longer content with the constitutional prohibitions on governmental control of faith, but rather sought to banish faith itself. Faith's submission to a higher moral imperative was a constant rebuke to the individual's self-interest, requiring suppression at all costs. Unencumbered by any morality supplied by faith in an active and present God, these secular roots gave rise to progressive thought and action. The divorce between "divine morality" and "reason" was framed as a battle for power over free will and thought. And it continues to this day.

Yet our founders chose our republican form of democracy for a reason. They fought hard for it. Our unique democracy was, and remains, the best earthly expression of the inevitable victory of God's superior morality over the corruption of secular despotism. Though not perfect (nothing is), it ideally prioritized life and our shared human dignity—sourced in the equality and freedom each of us receive as a creation of a loving God. Moreover, it provided the best possible hedge against the extremes of anarchy or totalitarianism, and the goal of each to destroy that unifying dignity.

ANARCHY V. TOTALITARIANISM

As applied to secular governance, extremes in the absence of this moral imperative can be demonstrated in the opposite or competing theories of anarchy (chaos) and totalitarianism (control). The examination of each is most easily understood from the individual's perspective—how he or she views themselves and their liberty relative to the world around them.

Anarchy

If, within Rousseau's paradigm, we were to measure personal freedom or liberty on a sliding scale, one side would correspond to the complete lack of restraint inherent in an individual having ceded none of his or her natural freedom to the whole. A totally free society, then, would be one in which the individual is in no way morally or legally bound to respect the natural or civil freedom (or rights) of anyone else. There would be no compromised civil freedom—no contractual consensus. Whatever is moral and right would be dictated solely by one's own relative sense of perfection or justice. Power therein would reside strictly with the individual.

Out of this lack of consensus, anarchy or chaos results, each of us in perpetual competition with one another in order to live. Such a society finds scientific expression in the Darwinian concept of natural selection or survival of the fittest, that the human being is simply a random product of nature adapting, evolving, for the sole purposes of surviving and propagating the species. Equilibrium within such chaos is found in the balance of life and death itself. The only truths are that we are born and then we die. All that exists in between is the individual's nihilistic[10] will to survive—to control their personal environment to ensure that survival.

Government, as an expression of that will, is the collective human effort to insert a relative sense of reason or order into that disorder and thereby alter or control the balance between life and death—preferably toward life. As noted above, the various forms of government are different expressions of how that power to control, or moral obligation, should be administered.

---

10. Generally, nihilism is a philosophy that eschews the existence of moral value and truth and asserts that life has no real meaning.

Totalitarianism

On the other side of the scale is totalitarianism: the complete restraint upon individuals who, having ceded all (or most) of their natural freedom to the whole (voluntarily or not), are completely subjugated by that power. Totalitarian regimes are authoritarian or dictatorial in nature, as found in entities with highly centralized power structures or bureaucracies such as those found in communism or fascism.

In the absence of any real liberty (or civil freedom), the only relevance of the individual is in the continued support and propagation of that system or regime and those who hold power, effectively rendering the individual a slave thereto. What is moral and right is dictated neither by God nor majority consensus, but rather by the individual or group of individuals at the top of those governmental structures/bureaucracies and imposed upon the rank and file through nonconsensual law and regulation, often enforced using methods designed to elicit compliance through fear or helplessness.

The reality is that most people desire the greatest amount of individual liberty possible. But living together requires cooperation—at least enough to avoid breaches of the peace. Therefore, the difference between anarchy and totalitarianism is the introduction of varying degrees of control, be it voluntary or involuntary, designed to address our human propensity to abuse our self-interest, and the friction that inevitably arises when that self-interest collides with the interests of others.

The more complex a society becomes, the more conflicts arise, the more we feel it necessary to increase the governmental response thereto in the form of law and regulation. But here is the catch: *the more law and regulation there is, the less free we are.* The less free we are, the less content we are. More conflicts arise. The resulting national disunity is self-perpetuating. We ignore Adam and Eve's painful lesson: law *is* slavery. In acquiescing thereto, and in the absence of personal accountability, we cede more and more of our individual liberty or freedom to the government for the sake of compelling cooperation. In so doing, we foster our own slavery to the law and to an increasingly powerful government.

A Compromise—Representative Democracy

Representative democracy is a compromise between the two political extremes, a means of balancing individual natural rights against the power of government. Ideally, at least in terms of a democracy, power is dispersed equally among its people as a check and balance against chaos on one side, and authoritarianism or control on the other, exercised—in our constitutional *republican* form of democracy—by proxies or representatives selected by the people to administer that power on their behalf.

The purpose of creating a representative system was to provide a means by which a greater number of citizens could participate in government. In a pure democracy direct participation in government by each individual citizen, in a growing nation, was logistically difficult given limitations of time and place—each and every decision requiring a referendum vote of all citizens. The election of representatives remedied that difficulty by extending equal power, or say, to those citizens whose views might, due to those limitations, go unexpressed.

This representative government is not an impersonal entity. In administering that cooperation, it reflects the values, both good and bad, of the individuals who are governed as well as those to whom the government has been entrusted. It must likewise account for the numerous ideological differences of those individuals. Though it theoretically responds impartially to the demands placed upon it, we know historically that politics prevail—because, after all, influence is power. Those seeking that power cater to blocs of those ideological differences. We have an innate need to be the master of that influence rather than its subject. It is a function of self-interest or preservation. Recalling C.S. Lewis's paradigm on good and its parasite, evil, that need or self-interest, left to its own devices, breeds immorality.

Our government, however, was not designed to function in a moral void. It can work as it should only when we are able to look inward and effectively acknowledge and deal with our natural inclination toward immoral self-interest. At the center of that introspection is the core belief about ourselves, our origin. It is fundamental to the way we view our relationships, including those that make up our government. The way in which we view our existence, either as products of random chance or as having been divinely created, dictates how we live and think and how we relate to one another practically and morally. It bears directly on how (and how well) we *voluntarily* cooperate with others and respect their rights.

In attributing our inalienable rights to our Creator, it is argued that our founders expressed a fundamental understanding about themselves, morality, and all of us as beings created by, and thus subordinate to, an omnipotent God: i.e., the "created" do *not* create the Creator. And within that Creator is something universally precious that no individual can influence or alter. To acknowledge God is, therefore, to acknowledge that we are not God.

This absolute is first and foremost an understanding about the natural order or hierarchy of all things, about life and our ultimate purpose. It influences every important decision we make because it provides the foundation upon which we all fall back when action is needed when facing the storms in our lives. As with Job's ordeal, this ancient fundamental truth seemingly influenced and ordered our founders' thoughts during the difficulties experienced in fashioning our government, considering that Darwin's scientific theories on creation and evolution were still seventy years away.

CHECKS AND BALANCES

The very structure of our government evidences the framers' understanding of this natural order. They specifically recognized the need to create a tripartite governmental framework through which the constitutional provisions for the separation of powers would account for our inherent imperfection or sin, i.e., our tendency toward unhealthy self-interest. We commonly know it as the system of checks and balances moderating the interaction between the three co-equal branches of government: executive, legislative, and judicial.

But for that inherent imperfection, there would be no logical reason or need for a system of "checks and balances." Since power is subject to abuse by those who hold it, the system's purpose was to separate or de-centralize that power to prevent any one branch (and thus the individuals within it) from consolidating power, dominating the others, or exerting undue influence in the administration of government's various functions.[11] Therefore,

11. In a current example of the checks and balances between the three branches of government, President Biden, claiming authority under the 2003 Heroes Act (H.R. 1412, Public Law 108–76), a law giving the Secretary of Education the limited ability to modify student loan repayments for military personnel engaged in active combat, raised similar concerns about separation of powers and executive overreach by unilaterally forgiving student debt to the tune of up to $400 billion, despite Congress's constitutional control over the nation's purse strings. A political act seemingly designed to influence young voters in the 2022 midterm elections, the President's appropriation of congressional function was struck down as invalid on June 30, 2023, in *Biden et al. v. Nebraska, et al.*, 600 U.S. ___ (2023), wherein Justice Roberts, writing for the majority, held that the Secretary overstepped that limited authority and opined that "[t]he Secretary's plan has "modified" the cited provisions only in the same sense that "the French Revolution 'modified' the

apart from creating efficiency by dividing up necessary governmental functions, the tripartite structure was designed to foster personal accountability in carrying out governmental duties in light of our individual imperfection.

While general consensus serves as lubrication for the operation of that secular tripartite government, undue self-interest (or immorality) stills renders the machine less efficient. An additive or catalyst is needed. The social contract explains well, in a secular sense, the technical arrangement and interaction of our rights and responsibilities to one another, but alone it minimizes or marginalizes the significance of God our Creator as the source of our inalienable rights and the centrality of that natural order or higher truth as a significant moderating factor in our interactions with others. Just as fear is the catalyst for division, the Christian's faith in the supremacy of God's love (or higher wisdom), and the internal change it produces in the individual's heart, is the counter-catalyst for unity, promoting humility, morality, and accountability in the actions carried out in furtherance of governmental duties.

As to the relevance of that internal change, Rousseau's "enlightened" understanding of the general consensus may well have been influenced by his observation of our egocentric or relative views about God, i.e., that "there [are] as many gods as there are people,"[12] implying that individuals do indeed define or create their own gods or faiths to suit themselves.[13] If God has no particular cooperative influence on our reason and interactions with others, this makes perfect sense. A morality flowing from such disparate beliefs could never, as quoted above, serve as "the supreme direction of the general will" for lack of any real consensus as to who God is or what, if anything, he does for us. Faith, then, in any form, could never provide a positive influence on our government, rendering those two institutions mutually exclusive. For the secularist or atheist, this is sufficient rational justification for their interpretation of the concept of separation of church and state.

Yet a value system that provides no *superior order* or absolutes, such as anarchy, is one that invites each of us to ultimately define our own truth and, hence, our own morality. Those things we choose to accept as true are most likely those that promote our own self-interests or those perceived as being essential for our personal survival—or at least our personal comfort

---

status of the French nobility"—it has abolished them and supplanted them with a new regime entirely." *Nebraska*, slip op. at 19–20.

12. Rousseau, *The Social Contract*, Book 4, Sec. 8.

13. "My own mind is my own church" (Paine, *The Age of Reason*, Part First, Sec. 1).

or image. Friction arises when those diverse interests invariably collide. Most of us accept the will of the people (the general consensus) in proscribing conduct we would otherwise condemn as being harmful to our society. We all trust that the collective wisdom of the people reflects our best interests (or at least the best interest of the majority), so we submit to it as the cost of living together in society. But there is such a thing as an immoral majority.[14] And in a declining democracy, the morality of that collective human wisdom is necessarily suspect.

In assessing the fairness of that collective wisdom or general will, there must be some ultimate standard by which it is measured. Most are content offering the consensus of our relative human law as that standard—the best we can do—as interpreted by judges. But laws are often enacted out of self-interest. And judges are merely human beings, as evidenced by the fact that even their judgments get overruled from time to time in an appellate process specifically designed to address human errors in judgment as to the application of the law. Sometimes Congress, as a check and balance, must intervene to change bad legal precedent.[15] After all, humans are imperfect,

14. Alexis de Tocqueville, the French political scientist and commentator on American democracy, observed a potential conflict within our democracy in what he termed the "tyranny of the majority," acknowledging that men do not change their innate character by uniting together into a majority, and the same self-interests by which they are united often work to deprive the minority of their rights, since there is nowhere else to turn but to that majority when those rights are abused. See de Tocqueville, "Unlimited Power of the Majority," accessed at https://xroads.virginia.edu/~Hyper/DETOC/1_ch15. htm. Institutionally, Tocqueville saw our nation's lack of centralized administration, i.e., the existence of local governmental entities, and the intercession of lawyers and jury trials as moderating influences on the majority's power, as he describes in the sixteenth chapter of his book.

15. One of our history's most noteworthy examples is the infamous decision in *Dred Scott v. Sandford*, 60 U.S. 393 (1857). Dred Scott, a black slave, sued for his freedom after being taken, along with his family, by Emerson, a previous owner, into Missouri, a state that prohibited slavery. There Emerson sold them all to Sandford, a New York citizen, who argued that Scott, being a slave, was not a citizen of Missouri. The U.S. Supreme Court agreed, holding that slaves were not considered citizens under the Constitution and therefore had no standing to sue (i.e., the federal government lacked jurisdiction to hear the case). After the slavery issue was settled by the Civil War, Congress adopted both the Civil Rights Act of 1866 and the Fourteenth Amendment to the Constitution in 1868, giving citizenship to all African Americans and thus equal protection under the law. Clearly, the secular human law tolerated, even promoted, slavery—treating a fellow human being as chattel (property). But the ultimate source of the will to banish it arose, not out of the fallible secular consensus that had long turned a blind eye to slavery out of self-interest, but from the superior *spiritual morality* infusing our God-given human rights to life, liberty, and the pursuit of happiness—and thus true freedom and equality.

influenced by circumstance and self-interest. But again, what is the perfect standard? The legal assessment of our human rights invariably boils down to issues of morality.

Our inalienable rights are born in God's divine morality. The Christian believers among our founders understood that our existence, as creations of God, is subject to God's sovereignty and superior wisdom; it is God who, as our Creator and sovereign, endows us with our rights. Today, however, our rights are simply those items of self-interest we choose to assert without reference to any foundation in objective morality or truth. They are expressed, like much in our age of social media, as fickle popular trends. Life, liberty, and the pursuit of happiness are conducted without reference to any sovereign authority higher than ourselves. In the process, the core moral value of our Constitution is substantially weakened.

Morality influences how our freedom and equality, our rights, are administered. Morality created from human reason—or the relative secular consensus—differs markedly from the organic morality derived from a perfect God and perfect Law. Morality with respect to God deals with our obedience to his perfect Law and the effect of that obedience on our imperfect relationships with others. Morality derived from secular consensus is self-derived, relative and flexible, managed by those in power, an imperfect rule guiding imperfect relationships.

Our egocentric nature demands that we see ourselves as good. And in our vanity we must project that image. We do not wish to appear evil or self-interested to others. In order to justify and sustain our own positive self-image and avoid accusations of hypocrisy, we must necessarily concede that all mankind is primarily good and that the general will to which we conform must itself be "good"—or, at least, good enough; otherwise no one would willingly submit to it.

The Christian perspective is just the opposite. It plainly admits that our nature is inherently sinful or "bad" and the will to which we voluntarily submit (and thus the law and regulation, or government, flowing from that will) is corrupted by that nature. Consequently, something more is needed to counter that negative influence, something that enriches and elevates our secular justice. For the believing Christian that "something more" is fully expressed in one act of perfect humility, submission, and love: Christ's willing sacrifice on the cross.

In light of that sacrifice the reader might reasonably ask, which is better, a government comprised of individuals whose goal is to find a relative consensus apt to be skewed by self-interest, favoring those with the power and money to exert influence, or a government comprised of those whose priority is to unify in humility, so as to place the interests of others before themselves, as did Christ?

7

A Higher, Perfect Order

IT IS ARGUED THAT the inherent freedom and equality each of us receives as the creation of an active and present God moderates the application of that self-interest much more so than any equality we could ever obtain by relinquishing (voluntarily or begrudgingly) some of our natural freedom for the sake of the "general will."

Inherent freedom is absolute. It cannot be usurped by anyone, regardless of power. Freedom and equality based strictly on submission to the general consensus is relative, subject to the inevitable differences in power and influence exercised by individuals or blocs within that general will. Under God's perfect Law, we are all equally accountable. Under the relative general will, we are not. Accountability gets lost in the vagaries of bureaucracy and in the corrupted power structure.

Some politicians, impervious to the application of the law, say and do whatever they wish regardless of truth, diminishing the efficacy of the law. Two systems of justice are created in the process—one for them and one for everyone else. Nothing denigrates our democracy more than the hypocrisy of entitled politicians refusing to take responsibility for anything—unless it benefits them personally. We entrust our power to those elected politicians. To wield that power without accountability is an abuse of that trust.

It is sinful human nature to abuse that trust, to take advantage of or hide behind the political machine. As that machine grows to accommodate ever-expanding policies and programs instituted as a result of our lack of

The Prime Law

accountability, it absorbs more individuals to hide behind. In the process those with power wield it artfully, behind a bureaucratic veil, until such time as that power can no longer be questioned or controlled by the general will. It is an authoritarian regime in the making.

This is not the transparency our founders intended. They took a step back from themselves, acknowledging God as the source and facilitator of our government. During the Federal Convention in June 1787, even the aforementioned statesman, Benjamin Franklin, the "Deist," revealed his true pragmatic heart when offering this encouragement in an effort to institute daily prayer to help the delegates work through the rancor that had stalled progress in the debates:

> In this situation of this assembly, groping, as it were, in the dark, to find political truth, and scarce able to distinguish it when presented to us, how has it happened, sir, that we have not hitherto once thought of humbly applying to the Father of lights to illuminate our understandings? In the beginning of the contest with Great Britain, when we were sensible of danger, we had daily prayer in this room for the divine protection. Our prayers, sir, were heard, and they were graciously answered. All of us who were engaged in the struggle must have observed frequent instances of a superintending Providence in our favor. To that kind Providence we owe this happy opportunity of consulting in peace on the means of establishing our future national felicity. And have we forgotten that powerful Friend? Or do we imagine that we no longer need His assistance? I have lived, sir, a long time and the longer I live the more convincing proofs I see of this truth: *that God governs in the affairs of men.* And if a sparrow cannot fall to the ground without his notice,[1] is it probable that an empire can rise without His aid? We have been assured, sir, in the sacred writings that "except the Lord build the house, they labor in vain that build it."[2] I firmly believe this and I also believe that without His concurring aid, we shall succeed in this political building no better than the builders of Babel.[3] We shall be divided by our little partial local interests; our projects will be confounded; and we ourselves shall become a reproach and by-word down to future ages.[4] And, what is worse,

---

1. See Matt 10:29, "Are not two sparrows sold for a penny? Yet not one of them will fall to the ground outside your Father's care."

2. See Ps 127.

3. See Gen 11:1–9.

4. See Ezek 5:14. See also Governor Winthrop's similar words above, page 10, n. 1.

mankind may hereafter, from this unfortunate instance, despair of establishing governments by human wisdom, and leave it to chance, war, and conquest.

I therefore beg leave to move that, henceforth, prayers imploring the assistance of Heaven, and its blessings on our deliberations, be held in this assembly every morning before we proceed to business, and that one or more of the clergy of this city be requested to officiate in that service.[5]

In his own words, Mr. Franklin ironically revealed the vulnerability of secular or enlightened human "reason" and the beneficial influence of the "Father of lights" (the illuminator of truth) upon that reason, to whom he encouraged the delegation to turn *in faith* at that difficult time. His numerous references to Christian Scripture in support (Old and New Testament alike) indicates that his knowledge or study of the faith and of Christ's divinity was perhaps deeper or more incisive than his later 1790 correspondence to Ezra Stiles, quoted above, would lead one to believe.[6] Despite his Deism he admitted that *"God governs in the affairs of men."* God did have *current* relevance and application in our lives! God's nature *was knowable* in his availability to unite us in times of real need and in his ability to influence outcomes.

Surely Franklin could not trust in the benevolence of that influence without first having the faith to believe that God or Providence, whoever he/it is, is in fact benevolent and cares about us. He admitted that God's intercession influenced the successful outcome of the war against England. Apart from answered prayer to which Franklin refers (the external manifestations of God's common grace), the best earthly evidence we have of God's benevolence is in the words and actions of Jesus Christ himself—and in our personal salvation and faith (the internal manifestation of God's special grace).

Franklin's duality—his apparent ability to compartmentalize—mirrors so many of us in our lack of commitment to faith: one part of us content in the sufficiency of our human reason, and the other part hoping there is something more when that human reason or effort fails to yield desired results. In other words, when all else fails, then, and only then, do we turn to God and pray.

---

5. Madison, *Debates in the Federal Convention of 1787*, 147, accessed at http://www.thefederalistpapers.org/wp-content/uploads/2012/12/Debates-in-the-Federal-Convention-of-1787.pdf. (Emphasis and references added).

6. See Franklin quote, chapter 3.

Without a foundation fortified with the unalterable, eternal Spirit of our Creator—a higher perfect order—the nation rests solely upon an ever-shifting human consensus influenced by the subjectivity of secular human reason, the transparency of which is often clouded by circumstance and self-interest. Even Franklin saw, in the absence of God's higher morality, the "despair of establishing governments by human wisdom." Given the extraordinary animosity and gridlock in today's government, Mr. Franklin's plea has poignant relevance. The difference here is that the Christian does not wait for life's inevitable impasses to occur before seeking the perfect Creator's wisdom. It is available to us all, right now.

AN OMNI-PERFECT GOD

That Creator's nature is often expressed in the combination of three attributes: he is omniscient, omnipresent, and omnipotent. But there is a fourth. The Christian God is "omni-perfect": limitlessly perfect in his being, his power, his love, his mercy, his grace, and his justice. Jesus[7] himself exhorts us to "be perfect, therefore, as your heavenly Father is perfect."[8] How on earth can one be as perfect as God? Left to ourselves, we cannot. Despite our self-serving assertions to the contrary, *compared to God* we are not primarily good.

The Parable of the Rich Ruler

> A certain ruler asked [Jesus], "Good teacher, what must I do to inherit eternal life?"
>
> "Why do you call me good?" Jesus answered. "No one is good—except God alone. You know the commandments: 'You shall not commit adultery, you shall not murder, you shall not steal, you shall not give false testimony, honor your father and mother.'"
>
> "All these I have kept since I was a boy," he said.
>
> When Jesus heard this, he said to him, "You still lack one thing. Sell everything you have and give to the poor, and you will have treasure in heaven. Then come, follow me."
>
> When he heard this, he became very sad, because he was very wealthy. Jesus looked at him and said, "How hard it is for the

7. Jesus Christ, the physical incarnation of the Christian triune God (God on earth).
8. Matt 5:48.

rich to enter the kingdom of God! Indeed, it is easier for a camel to go through the eye of a needle than for someone who is rich to enter the kingdom of God."

Those who heard this asked, "Who then can be saved?"

Jesus replied, "What is impossible with man is possible with God."[9]

"Why do you call me good? . . . No one is good—except God alone." In another attempt to separate Christ from his divinity, many discredit the deep truth of this lesson by insisting that Jesus's own response proves that he is not God. But the parable has little to do with the issue of Jesus's divinity, or lack thereof. It is about the nature of the ruler's relationship with his power and wealth. Jesus, being fully both God and man[10], could have answered him in any way and from any perspective he wished. But Jesus took the wealthy ruler—as he does all of us—as he found him, at the point in his life that prompted the inquiry, and spoke to him in terms he would understand. The ruler, expecting an answer from a wise man, got exactly what he asked for and exactly what he needed.

Seeking instruction on how to be good enough to enter heaven, the wealthy ruler addressed Jesus respectfully as "good teacher." Stepping into the perspective of the man before him, the first thing the Teacher did in answering the question was to deftly reorient the man's relative perspective on goodness from "man" to "God." Entry into heaven is not a relative exercise in comparative good or a function of our altruism. It is a spiritual exercise in obedience to God's perfect Law—a function of salvation. Jesus wanted the man to assess his "goodness" not as to others, a relative standard, but rather against God's perfection.

In so doing, Jesus forced the man to reconsider his priorities: his love of position, wealth, and power or his love of God, because his perspective influenced his actions. The man wanted heaven on his own terms. We all do. Though he claimed to have lived a righteous life since he was a boy, Jesus exposed that righteousness, while perhaps even well-meant, as superficial. The price for this God's heaven was everything the man had—like Job, *everything that God had given him.* The thought of having to part with his power and wealth in order to obtain eternal life was a major stumbling block. He could not serve both God and his power and wealth.[11]

9. Luke 18:18–27. See also Matt 19:16–26; Mark 10:17–27.

10. "For in Christ all the fullness of the Deity lives in bodily form." (Col 2:9).

11. See Matt 6:24.

Only after one first comes to that conclusion does Jesus then provide turning to God as the solution. The man could not understand that what Christ was asking him to do was to subordinate his personal sovereignty to that of God's—to commit his wealth and power not to himself, but, with the tools God had provided, to the kingdom of God.

Like the wealthy ruler, the intellectual, political, and financial elite often claim to use the benefit of their advantage to lift others out of their disadvantage—to prove that they are doing something noble. Often it is a means of spinning or justifying class distinctions. Many would rather act paternally, directing from above from their positions of relative power and security, rather than personally sacrificing their advantage in order to enter the actual realm of the disadvantaged.[12] Some might even (and often do) expect a quid pro quo for their benevolence. Darwin would surely agree. Advantage means survival.

None of us are immune to the lure of that security—that safe haven. If we have it, we are, like the rich ruler, loath to give it up. If we do not, we strive to obtain it. We all want to be in that position—to be able to help from above (or not). It is God-like. Jesus, however, did exactly that. He voluntarily relinquished his unlimited power, his life, all for the sake of sinners like us. And that is who this wealthy ruler was speaking to—the very icon of that ultimate sacrifice. There was no higher authority, no superior power or law, no better teacher, no better example.

The salvation Jesus offered was the only way to rectify that systemic inequality—between the man and those for whom he, as a wealthy ruler, was responsible. The ruler's goodness was meaningless in the absence of his submission to God, and his acknowledgment that whatever good he had was sourced in God's grace—not in his own power. It is the same for all of us today. While we may not be required to give up our wealth and power, we should be willing to do so if necessary. It is a question of will. Are we willing to do what is required of us for the benefit of others—to subordinate that wealth and power to the superior Law of God?[13]

---

12. This "not-in-my-backyard" hypocrisy was recently revealed, for example, by politicians in New York; Washington, DC; and Chicago, excoriating the governor of Texas for providing transportation for illegal aliens to those cities. Because of their benevolent images as "sanctuary cities," one would think that they would welcome these disadvantaged individuals with open arms. But that was not the case, as they were forced to realize and share in the overwhelming social and fiscal burdens reckless border policies have placed on the citizens of Texas and other border states.

13. "My command is this: Love each other as I have loved you. Greater love has no

Witnessing the hard lesson, those around Jesus asked, "Who then can be saved?" He answered, "What is impossible with man is possible with God." The point Jesus was making is that there is nothing we can do on our own to comply with God's standard of perfection. There is no scale upon which we can hope that our good deeds outweigh the bad. Our entry into God's kingdom is not a 51-percent proposition—striving to produce that one last act of goodness that will tip the scale and propel us through the pearly gates.

It has nothing at all to do with us, or how we choose to use our individual power, but *everything* to do with a perfect righteousness that has been *imputed to us* through the agency of a perfect third party—Jesus Christ, our proxy in faith—to whom God opens our hearts. Only the perfect could accomplish what the imperfect could not. For Franklin, the providence of a perfect God could accomplish what their imperfect convention seemingly could not—the unification of diverse parties and interests toward a common beneficial goal through submission in prayer.

Just as it did for our founders' deliberative process, the infusion of that Spirit or higher order fortifies the process of voting as the power of consensus—the best expression of our relative freedom and equality. The founders understood that the process must not be abused to subvert the very nature of the democracy they sought to create. Otherwise democracy is simply a malleable, relative ideal, changeable at the whim of those in power. Today the issue is exposed by those who view our federal Constitution and its principles as constantly evolving—revealing the frighteningly real potential for evolving us right out of our democracy.

Yet the very first amendment to our Constitution, for example, also guarantees freedom of religion[14]—which, for the believing Christian, rec-

---

one than this: to lay down one's life for one's friends." —Jesus Christ. (John 15:12–13).

14. The "Establishment/Free Exercise Clause" of the Constitution states, "Congress shall make no law respecting an establishment of religion, or prohibiting the free exercise thereof; or abridging the freedom of speech, or of the press; or the right of the people peaceably to assemble, and to petition the Government for a redress of grievances" (U.S. Const. amend. I). Congress enacting laws establishing religion is quite different from the government expressing support thereof. Compare this to early New England colonial government, which enacted laws requiring the collection of taxes to support the church. Leaders like Roger Williams were set off from those early colonies in part over disagreement with such laws, believing that it was not the government's place to force the support of one faith over another—showing favoritism in the process (a form of inequality)—and thereby effectively establishing a national religion. While such laws clearly demonstrated the priority the colonists placed on faith, it just as clearly constituted a restraint on free

ognizes that the only perfection that exists is that which resides in God himself—the very source of the self-evident truths or rights our Constitution protects. True morality, and thus transparency, arises from that omni-perfect, non-evolving, superior order from which nothing may be hidden. That rock-solid order, as expressed in the Christian's freedom of religion, is the anchor that prevents our democracy—and our freedom—from being swept away by changing social or political tides.

---

thought and worship. It placed bureaucracy between the individual and God, the very same problem Martin Luther saw in the church and was arguing to reform.

8

Faith and Humility
Not Intellect

THE PROOF OF GOD, then, is not in a changed world but in the humility of one changed heart—not the external but the internal. In our hubris we demand that God stand before us and prove himself by healing the problems of our world before we will deem him worthy of consideration in our own lives. We hypocritically blame God for his failure to step in and remedy our misdeeds in vain, childish attempts to shift accountability and avoid consequences. The world was given to us, like gods with free will, to either cherish or destroy—to choose heaven or hell. Our individual and collective abuse of the power given to us evidences our choice. In our lack of humility we seem bent on destroying this world. God has supplied us with the tools we need to cherish it, but using them accountably, as useful members of his kingdom, is up to us.

That kingdom is to be found within all who, in faith, have humbly submitted to it. Faith will never be found solely through the application of reason. There is no shortage of public debate among academics about the existence of God, all discussed in the language of science and reason. Establishing the existence of God and God's morality using reason is an art—an argument discipline known as apologetics. It is a means of applying logic and reason to explain and support the spiritual. It can be a very effective tool and does have its place—admittedly, even in this work.

One of the goals of apologetics is to introduce or awaken the rational mind to the spiritual heart, thereby leading to critical self-examination. But in the inability to comprehend or express the spiritual, faith is often over-intellectualized and its substance invariably lost in the weeds of sociology, psychology, or arcane theology. The languages of spirit and reason are quite different, not in how they are spoken, but rather in the place from which they are heard. It is the difference between the heart and the mind.

Faith is to accept something our reason cannot fully comprehend—without necessarily knowing the answer. That ability to accept the unknown is not a function of reason that strives to rationalize and explain; instead, it is a function of love. Love, by its very nature, strives to accept. It is divine. It is *revealed*, not discovered. History proves our innate need to dominate and control. Thus, even if science and reason established the existence of God or the nature of God's power, it would still not impart the wisdom that is the heart of God's truth—a truth that only he reveals. We seek God's power, not the wisdom of his truth, separating divinity and morality in the process. In our lack of humility, God's truth is simply one more perceived subjugation to overcome. In overcoming that truth, we are free to create our own.

Transformational knowledge of God's truth comes not through the application of our intellect or reason but from God's direct revelation to the individual. He awakens an internal spiritual desire, a willingness to meet him at that place we need to be in order to receive or hear it. The value of apologetics is in introducing individuals to that place—that possibility. But the skeptic who demands external proof will never find God or fully grasp his truth because it is revealed only *inside* the individual who first submits to it—*an act of humility*. It is then followed by the faith to see where that submission, that act of love, leads.

ARMINIANISM V. CALVINISM

Where does this desire or submission originate—in our own initiative or God's will? It is an age-old question over which truly superior minds have, for centuries, disagreed. This researcher's brief observations are inserted here merely to acquaint the reader generally with this subject, one made complex by an inability to comfortably reconcile secular and spiritual definitions of free will. The nature of that desire/submission, however, is important because it goes to the very heart of the destructive influence of relativism on Christian morality and, thus, our humility.

Jacobus Arminius

Jacobus Arminius (1569–1609) argued, generally,[1] that God offers salvation to all—that he initiates a strong, persuasive suggestion in our hearts through the power of the Holy Spirit (what is known as prevenient grace or partial regeneration), but that our acceptance of that suggestion (for purposes of completing that regeneration—or, salvation) is an act of human free will. Arminius's position was a rejection of *predestination*, a core concept of John Calvin's Reformed theology (discussed below) asserting, based upon his reading of Scripture,[2] that a person's salvation was predetermined by God before the world began, a determination that the individual could not ultimately resist. Salvation was, for Calvin, not a matter of free will, but an irresistible act of God's special grace.

Eschewing predestination, Arminianism holds that God did not pre–choose those whom he would save before the world began, but that he merely foresaw those who would choose him. As an act of free will, this choice could be forfeited by subsequent sin. Therefore, people could choose, as an act of free will, to accept God's gift of salvation, and by that same free will, lose it by continuing to sin thereafter.

Under the Arminian view it seems, then, that if acceptance and loss are both matters of free will, it follows that, provided God's invitation was a constant, a person could choose, and then lose, salvation as many times as they, in their free will, desired. Whether at the end of the day they were saved or not would be a function of timing—that one died on a day occurring in the period in which they had chosen salvation. This uncertainty of result would tend to prove that our free will is indeed imperfect.

---

1. There are differing interpretations of Arminianism, beyond the scope of this basic review, which seemingly adjust or moderate its application given the complexities of the issue of free will.

2. See Rom 8:29–30: "For those God foreknew he also predestined to be conformed to the image of his Son, that he might be the firstborn among many brothers and sisters. And those he predestined, he also called; those he called, he also justified; those he justified, he also glorified."

See also Eph 1:4–7:

> For he chose us in him before the creation of the world to be holy and blameless in his sight. In love he *predestined* us for adoption to sonship through Jesus Christ [emphasis added], in accordance with his pleasure and will—to the praise of his glorious grace, which he has freely given us in the One he loves. In him we have redemption through his blood, the forgiveness of sins, in accordance with the riches of God's grace.

Either that or the rule must be, once lost, it is lost for all time without hope of ever regaining that status. If true, no one could ever be saved because we all continue to sin—even after salvation. We are not perfect. But the difficulty of this view of uncompelled free will is that it seems to inadvertently reinforce the influence of sin, while undermining the power and effect of God's perfect grace and Christ's sacrifice—his substitution—for permanently remediating that sin.

Further, as with the works-justification issue discussed above about how much "good" is enough for obtaining salvation, the question then becomes, how much sin, or "bad," is enough to lose it? We then find ourselves in a further academic debate over the relative quality of various sins—some being more "sinful" than others. This, in turn, leads to the relative exercise, or error, of comparing ourselves not to God, but to each other. In order to minimize our culpability for that sin, we invariably ask, how bad was it compared to that of another? But what is the standard used for making that determination, our own or God's?

Relative Sin

The core of this essay's perspective on both faith and government is the individual's salvation experience. That experience leads not only to beneficial spiritual change, but to a larger positive social and political change through our understanding of God's superior love and its influence on our love for ourselves and others (The Prime Law).

It is difficult to imagine a more effective way to infuse disunity into that experience, or even the orderly operation of the faith, than by opening it up to arguments about varying degrees of sin or various ways to view it. We saw what happened when Satan manipulated God's Law to induce Eve to eat the fruit despite God's admonition not to eat it. It was all downhill from there. Yet we simply cannot shed that need to manipulate God's Law in order to affect a beneficial personal outcome. For reasons of expediency we wash Scripture in the pool of relative human reason simply to justify our actions—to create exceptions to the rule. But either we believe in the inerrancy and, thus, primacy of God's Law, or we do not.

We are all sinners regardless of degree. That sin—regardless of degree—separates us from God and his kingdom. Still, we try so hard to carve out that home in a place we neither fully understand nor truly love, without the willingness to conform to it, because for many it is not about salvation,

God's kingdom, or his will, it is about the desire to obtain a perceived benefit—the benefit of eternal life without the cost of accepting God's Law.

Complete forgiveness and eternal life are certainly desirable things. But we want them on our own terms without having to change. Like those who interpret the Constitution as evolving, for many God's Law is not set in stone but is merely a set of general guidelines. To make it comfortable, we can tailor that faith, those requirements, to suit our preferences or image. The easiest way to avoid conforming to that Law is by relativizing sin and constructing exceptions, thereby redirecting the comparison of ourselves not to God, but to each other.

Relative sin is a concept that applies strictly to God, not man. As a matter of ultimate judgment and punishment we have nothing at all to say about it. Recall Jesus's response to Pilate after being told that he had the power to either free or crucify him. Jesus responded that Pilate would have no power over him had Pilate not received it from above and that, therefore, the one who handed Jesus over to Pilate was guilty of a greater sin.[3]

Jesus was not comparing one sin, or sinner, to another for purposes of assessing their current situation so they could argue about it among themselves as to who was more culpable. Rather, it was a chilling preview of the parties' future. As the comment was given in the context of "power from above," he was revealing to Pilate God's authority and power to judge and punish sins according to his own will—his ultimate justice and mercy. Indeed, both Pilate and Caiaphas would face punishment for abusing the power given to them by God. Its severity, however, would be determined solely by that power above when the appropriate time for judgment arrived. The idea that any one of us could manipulate God's ultimate judgment of our actions for a more advantageous result is the epitome of self-deception.

God determines the ultimate, eternal punishment for sin. Church consensus/leadership does neither. Outside that context the perspective on sin and salvation changes from God's prerogative, or will, to the individual's or group's desire for a particular outcome. They become political matters, a comparative tool used to insert relative human reason into a purely spiritual matter—to justify a desired result or shape policy within the church.

For us, in the here and now, salvation is dispositive of the issue of sin. Punishment for sin is a problem only for the unsaved—those who have not accepted God's sovereignty and Christ's invitation for salvation. That too is strictly God's realm, not ours. That is why, in this writer's opinion, Christian

---

3. See the conversation between Jesus and Pilate related in chapter 5.

salvation cannot be a function of uncompelled free will. Sin taints our free will. As a result, we cannot apply that imperfect free will to our salvation—an act of God's perfect grace.

There is another view on salvation, however, that renders relative sin and comparisons to each other moot. It is the view offered by a sixteenth-century Reformed theologian who believed that if we are new individuals in Christ—through the grace of God's salvation experience—we are completely forgiven regardless of the "degree" of sin. And that forgiveness cannot be taken away.

John Calvin

John Calvin (1509–1564), the father of the Puritans' faith, believed that the human heart is irremediably sinful and that the individual is saved by God's grace alone, through faith in Christ. Unlike the Arminian view discussed above, basic Reformed Christian doctrine advocates that God predetermines the individual's salvation. It is his choice, not ours. The individual cannot ultimately resist that predetermination. It is not an act of pure free will. God's call to salvation is an irresistible act of special grace upon the individual. To those individuals who are predestined, God's inserts within them a deep, painful awareness of, and remorse for, their sin—and a desire to repent. Along with it, he provides the ability—the faith—to do so by believing in his son, Jesus Christ, as the means of redemption for those sins. With that belief, the individual realizes God's special grace by accepting the salvation Christ offers. God's special grace is fulfilled, therefore, not through our own will, but through Jesus Christ.[4]

From the Calvinist perspective the issue is not simply whether God has fettered our free will by interfering with our ability to "freely" choose him and, hence, our salvation, but rather that our free will is already fettered by our sin and we are, as a result, incapable of making that choice. As a prisoner of, or slave to, that sin, we cannot free ourselves.

Once saved, however, the individual is saved for all time. The price paid by Christ's sacrifice covers all one's sins, past, present, and future. An

---

4. After Satan caused Eve to sin in Eden, God, referring to Jesus Christ, said to him, "I will put enmity between you and the woman, and between your offspring and hers; *he* will crush your head, and you will strike his heel (emphasis added)." (Gen 3:15). That enmity is Jesus Christ—his intercession for sinners; the manifestation or promise of God's grace.

individual continuing to live a life of deliberate, unrepentant sin after apparent salvation would be evidence that the individual never experienced salvation in the first place. Despite our eternal estate in God's kingdom being assured, no doubt all individuals will, to some extent, continue to sin, or err, after salvation. Our human nature is, and always will be in this life, imperfect. The practical difference here, in this life, is its scope and how the individual deals with it once guided by the indwelling Holy Spirit (a gift of God's grace), knowing that that sin has already been atoned for and we are, thereafter, free from its eternal penalty.

Free Will

The issue remains: what, then, is free will? From a purely secular perspective, it is helpful to distinguish between the natures of various actions. For example, we can choose to make any sandwich we like and eat it, the motivation being that we are hungry and need to eat. We may even enjoy it. We can choose to dye our hair green, the motivation being the desire to look different or to be unique. Such choices really have no moral imperative per se. They are simply things we voluntarily do at any given time without injurious effect either to ourselves or others.

But a different issue arises when those choices adversely affect ourselves or others. When we overindulge in that sandwich, the motivation or *reason* for eating it changes. Enjoyment and nutrition (the good) becomes harmful gluttony or obsession (the bad). Likewise, if we were to demand that others eat the same sandwich, the beneficial desire to share (goodwill) becomes an arbitrary need to control (ill will). The same would apply to compelling another to dye their hair green in order to conform to one's image or ideology.

As earlier noted by C.S. Lewis, those things enabling someone who is bad to be bad, are in themselves good things.[5] There is something in all of us that can flip from good to bad every beneficial attribute we have. That something is our innate sin. The Calvinist would argue, therefore, that as to moral decisions, including the matter of our salvation, we really do not have unfettered free will because our inherently sinful nature precludes it. We are not perfect. If we were, we would always make the right (or righteous) choice. But, clearly, we do not. The fact that we do not evidences well our propensity to sin.

5. See the Lewis quote in the Introduction.

Forcing our choice—or will—on someone else implicates secular morality because it attempts to define or order our relationship with that other person. In varying degrees, it interferes with their freedom. Still, our interactions with others necessarily entail a certain amount of permissive give and take—or clash of wills—to which we all submit. Together, as a society, we define the limits of that permission by imposing secular law—necessary for maintaining order. As explained by Rousseau, we submit to that imposition as a reasonable, consensual cost of participating therein. Misusing that will or power in order to manipulate others, however, exceeds the scope of that individual or collective permission. In harming ourselves, we likewise exceed that collective permission by damaging our individual value to society. In either case our accountability to that society is breached.

Yet as the secular government or state adjusts our accountability by adjusting law, not only does it alter the morality of the actions we take in the exercise of our will toward others, but it alters its own morality in controlling that will. A growing autocracy panders to society by hypocritically espousing the value of the individual, and individual "rights", while manipulating the law to the point where it is no longer accountable to that individual. This is why an immoral government tolerates social unrest (rioting, vandalism, looting, etc.) as a diversion or blind to the process of consolidating greater power in itself.

It is a transitional process. When people are too busy hating others, they really have no time to consider the larger motivations of those seeking or exercising power behind the scenes. So much effort is expended in trying to distract and devalue the individual and, hence, that will because that is where ultimate power lies. Mutual accountability between individual and state is lost. Individual value and will is rendered irrelevant to the superior will of the state and those controlling it, i.e., authoritarianism.

Only the will of the *individual* can prevent this from happening. That will—those grass roots—must somehow be reinforced, perfected. Accountability for the believing Christian goes much deeper than the *act* of exercising our will in a morally acceptable way as defined by relative secular law. The individual is first accountable to God and God's absolute love—that Prime Law that defines our relationships, first with him and then with others. Christian morality is our obedience to God and God's love. Secular morality is our obedience to the relative rule of law. There is no love in the secular rule of law. Applying secular law with relative fairness is not the same as applying it with love.

Thus spiritual obedience informs our secular accountability. The Christian's imperfect will, fortified by God's wisdom and grace, is better equipped to stand up to the sinful propensity to take advantage of, or be taken advantage of by, others. The effect of God perfecting us vicariously through the sacrifice of Jesus Christ—in forgiving our sins—is to liberate our fettered free will to which we were slaves, enabling us to lead more righteous lives—to love others. Sharing God's love is the ultimate expression of our emancipated free will.[6]

In that transition, the Christian understands that the real wall between church and state is the beneficial effect of their faith on moral individual will—the protective barrier between our individual God-given power and rights and the will of an immoral, self-interested government. This is the appropriate context of the individual's First Amendment religious liberty.[7] The Bill of Rights provided limitations upon the power of the federal government over states and individuals—designed therefore not to protect the government from the people, but to protect the citizens from an imperious government.

That is the perspective abused by those seeking larger government control. The government, however, is not a distinct entity apart from the people. The people *are* the government and the source of government's power. The picture of disunity examined above substantiates the massive scale of the people's mutual failure of will and, hence, government's performance as a reflection of that failure. We clearly choose to act in conformance with the desires of our sinful nature. We understand from Christ's call to perfection that our free will is slave to and thus "fettered" by that inclination. This is why Scripture exclaims that we are all slaves to that parasite, sin.[8] In that slavery we cede our authority to that imperious government.

For the Christian, there is no greater moral issue than salvation because it re-orders our relationship with God and, hence, each other. The Prime Law has no application to our lives until God is an integral part of those relationships. Yet our sinful nature renders us incapable of freely making

6. Some scholars claim, however, that free cannot technically exist because fee will is a means of self–definition, and that the only entity truly able to self–define is God. Ultimately, as his creations, God defines us. To the extent that we might view love as being sourced entirely in God's grace—rather than independently in our free will—there is some logic to the argument.

7. The Bill of Rights and the First Amendment may be examined online at https://www.archives.gov/founding-docs/bill-of-rights-transcript.

8. See John 8:34.

that righteous choice. We need help. Therefore, it is only by God's grace that we are saved, by *faith* in Jesus Christ.[9] We are aided in that faith—in making the righteous choice—by God's Holy Spirit, *his will.* Thereafter, if actions conceived in our free will glorify God by conforming to the Prime Law, we enter into that will. If not, God's perfect will is done regardless.

Free will and morality are complex issues. They are presented here only in the broadest of terms, as viewed by this writer, to help the reader consider them in the larger context of the arguments being advanced in this work. That said, in the deep search for God's ultimate truth in all things, we risk creating more division than unity, evidencing our lack of humility and our human need not simply to know and understand but to be right. The desire for a more perfect obedience can become, like it was for the religious Pharisees, a legalistic act of works, not submission in love.

Only an insecure, faithless person demands that the other prove that love. People can know in their hearts that they love, and they can say loving words and do loving acts, but therein love is merely inferred, not proved. It is only *circumstantial* evidence. There may, in fact, be an ulterior motive to those loving acts other than love (e.g., personal advantage or other desires of our imperfect reason). Surely even the atheist believes in love, though it is doubtful they could prove it. They have likely experienced that sublime, fundamental change in their hearts and minds—a sober clarity and wisdom they know to be the truth but which they cannot really explain, other than to say it exists. Yet it is something to which they willingly submit. Love just is. There is no scientific predicate, equation, or formula for love. That is what makes love a *spiritual* matter. True love is not a product of our reason.

So it is with God and faith. We know it in our hearts. God is love. God places that love (his Spirit) in our hearts. That higher spiritual love is the core of God's Prime Law. It is a gift of his grace that cannot be demanded. In humbly seeking forgiveness for our lack of humility (our sin), it may only be requested.[10] That is the cost of admission. Materially it is absolutely free, but it does require spiritual submission. We must submit to that love. It is that ultimate spiritual paradox: freedom in submission, a sacrifice that pales considerably to the sacrifice Christ made to give us that opportunity.

9. See Eph 2:8–10.

10. "Ask and it will be given to you; seek and you will find; knock and the door will be opened to you. For everyone who asks receives; the one who seeks finds; and to the one who knocks, the door will be opened." (Matt 7:7–8).

That same spiritual paradox is reflected in our cooperative submission to the secular rule of law—that to be free, we must all submit to a higher authority. But to do so willingly is to invite critical self-examination. For some, this is a painful experience—one potentially evoking shame because in the end, if we are honest, we come to the clear realization that just as we cannot perfectly keep the law of God, neither can we perfectly keep the secular rule of law. We *all* fall short. Our hypocrisy lies in refusing to admit that in our innate inability to perfectly keep the law, we are, and always have been, sinners.

We should not underestimate the value of shame for just as it was for Job (and this writer as admitted in the Preface above), it is the painful reminder of our imperfect position relative to a perfect God. It is an important first step on the path to humility. There is no bargaining with God, no extenuating circumstances, no excuses. We are not revealing to God anything about ourselves that he does not already know. We cannot enlighten him about something he failed to grasp or consider regarding our intentions or situation. *Nothing* is hidden. The clothes we wear to hide our immorality are removed.

As with Job's dialogue with God, all that exists is the naked truth about who we really are. Painful as it is, it is appropriate to feel shame. If we allow that shame to do its work, we die in a sense to our imperfect selves, our sins. In accepting Jesus's substitutionary sacrifice for those sins, and in our willingness to submit to God's superior Law, we experience a rebirth,[11] a new canvas upon which God can begin his most excellent work in us. The only thing we lose is an unhealthy ego, exchanging it instead for a healthy humility.

That is the environment in which real change takes place. We humbly turn away from a selfish, unfulfilling life encumbered by the shame of our sins. And we reach out to others in a new spirit of love and cooperation. That love, and the actions we take in response, is nothing we need compare with, or answer to, that of others. Disunity rages on in the hypocritical demand for comparisons. Our response, and responsibility, is strictly a matter between ourselves and God. The removal of the divisive need to compare or prove ourselves to others is a gift of God's love. In adhering to the Prime Law to love him and others as ourselves—paying it all forward—class distinctions are utterly destroyed. That Law accomplishes what socialism/communism, or any other government, cannot: equality through love.

---

11. "Jesus replied, 'Very truly I tell you, no one can see the kingdom of God unless they are born again.'" (John 3:3).

A cause for celebration, this admission is a truly wondrous and most liberating event—our first step toward real, universal freedom. In that regenerated heart we see our potential and strength as individuals and as a nation. The shame abates in the forgiveness of our sins to which we are no longer slaves. We are truly free. In submitting to God's perfection, we become part of that perfection where slavery no longer exists. Our judgment is no longer clouded by the needs of the day. The path ahead is clear. A perfect God shows the way by speaking directly to our hearts, not by having his will imposed on us by a government of self-interest. Real truth and power reside in that internal dialogue.

Christianity, when properly understood and applied, allows us to fully discern and accept the distinction between the perfection of God's truth and the imperfection of the reality we create for ourselves. That faith provides us the motivation for persistently leading more righteous and productive lives despite our inability to perfectly keep the law. With that understanding we realize that an imperfect government can therefore *never* be our highest achievement. While each of us is free to pursue the liberties government preserves, government can never fulfill the role of a perfect God in our lives. Nor should it.

No government, group, or individual should purposely set up barriers to the attainment of this goal, barriers abundantly supplied in our own sin. Our founders made sure that our constitutional democratic republic is, by far, the form of government best able to absorb the competing interests comprising this nation, without ultimately interfering with the individual's free pursuit of happiness, truth, and meaning. Such freedom exists nowhere else in the world. For the believing Christian God's truth allows us to continually shine light on those dark aspects of ourselves and our government that would otherwise remain hidden. In the pursuit of becoming a more perfect union, this light reveals those things that need improvement or healing.

This is the whole point of the Christian faith: we can never be perfect, but we have a way to become "more perfect" in Christ. It is a spiritual pursuit, not an intellectual, social, or political pursuit. It is an act of faith and humility, not reason. If any of us had the power to make ourselves perfect—or save ourselves—then Christ's perfect sacrifice in humility would be rendered irrelevant and the Christian faith a sham. We would live in a self-made world in which we would all be gods, embracing survival of the fittest. Many, perhaps most, live as if this were true. But Jesus Christ admonished us all to be perfect, knowing that the God who sets the standard of perfection also supplies the means for its compliance—not through self-effort or free will, but through his grace.

9

Freedom and Equality
Gifts of God's Grace

WHAT IS GRACE? SIMPLY put, grace is an unmerited gift. Reformed Christianity posits two types of grace, common and special. Common grace is that aspect of God's creation that allows for good things. As to the environment in which we live, the beneficial sun, air, and rain and what they produce—the things that sustain us—are all gifts of common grace. As to our actions within that environment, even a bad person is capable of doing good things. They can love and have a family. They can assist the less advantaged. They can save a life. That common good is a general gift of God to humanity—despite our sinful nature.

One might explain common grace as God's protective restraint and balance in an imperfect world—that which saves humanity from falling into utter chaos. It sustains us all. The secularist or atheist would measure nature's goodness as matter of probabilities, and our desire to do good, not as a gift from God, but rather sourced in one's own sense of duty or altruism. But not everyone's sense of duty or altruism is the same. So clearly those actions are measured not by their own merit, but by one's own bias or preferences, or how they are perceived by others. Altruism, then, is always vulnerable to undue self-interest.

A sinner cannot, therefore, use that common grace to save themselves. Christian salvation is a transformation requiring something more. As noted above, it requires a gift from God directly to the individual. God, through *special* grace, calls an individual to salvation. He places within the individual sufficient faith to believe in him and in the power of Christ's atoning sacrifice for our sin. The eternal forgiveness of our sin and its penalty is the ultimate gift of God's special grace.

The price paid by Christ's sacrifice is sufficient to make us perfect in God's eyes because Jesus, as God incarnate, is perfect: "For by one sacrifice he [Christ] has made perfect forever those who are being made holy."[1] By faith and faith alone, we accept this imputed perfection or righteousness as our own—our salvation—a gift of God's perfect grace. From that one sincere act of faith and personal humility, our journey within God's kingdom begins—a continuing journey of being made more perfect, more holy. The Apostle Paul refers to this as the process of being "transformed by the renewing of [our minds]."[2] Therein we are "able to test and approve what God's will is—his good, pleasing *and perfect will*."[3]

In terms of our everyday actions, it is God's will against which we compare the application of our own will—rather than that of other people. In that process our minds are renewed and our hearts are regenerated. We grow in a wisdom that moderates our unrestricted thoughts and actions. That wisdom is the resolution of the tension between the heart and the mind, between emotion and logic, between faith and reason.

There is no just law conceived by man that is not already subsumed in the wisdom of God's perfect Law. Yet no human law, statute, regulation, or policy will ever effect lasting beneficial change in this world until the heart behind it changes. After all, government is a reflection of the heart of the people it serves. A corrupt government serves only itself. It displays the weight of sin on common grace. In the absence of a fixed moral center—in our faith—we cut our government adrift on the sea of relativism only to founder ineptly in self-interest. But the changed heart seeks to do justice because it has experienced firsthand God's ultimate gift of grace and love. Its receipt is indeed the infusion of the perfect into the imperfect.

The gift of special grace allows us to understand and more deeply appreciate God's common grace. Our special gift of imputed perfection changes all of our relationships, including those comprising government. The preoccupation with maneuvering for position and power in this life is revealed for what it is, empty, and completely useless in providing what we need most of all—hope. Not hope in something uncertain like a winning lottery ticket, but

1. Heb 10:14.
2. Rom 12:2.
3. Rom 12:2 (emphasis added).

the expectation and security we have in a vested guarantee. This gift produces an optimistic hope that draws us together and unifies us. It gives us the power to weather adversity because we know the ultimate outcome.

As in every relationship, a government filled with individuals grasping at life and power for their own sakes squanders that hope. The result is today's national despair and disunity. An ever-expanding government and its endless array of social and economic policies, created as panaceas for our social ills, are the secular corporate responses to that disunity. We enlarge the bureaucracy and increase its power by creating new government agencies, new laws, new policies, and new taxes to pay for them all—simply to mask our own failure of personal accountability.

In this regard the practical effect of the Christian founders' belief in a superior moral influence upon our unique democracy was to preserve greater individual freedom by providing the means for limiting the size and power of government and thereby the means for realizing true self-accountability. As to government, that will is expressed in the exercise of our most fundamental democratic freedom: the vote. This is the very cornerstone of our democracy, the means of preserving liberty and power within the people and not ceding it to the government by default for lack of self-control.

This is not to say that all government initiatives are inappropriate. They can be useful things—as with national security for example, one of our government's primary responsibilities given the state of this world.[4] In large expensive public initiatives, however, we tend to think we can do the greatest good. We can make an even greater impact for good, however, through our personal one-on-one relationships with others—each day—as God has with us, making a positive difference in one person's life. Together the cumulative effect of those individual efforts in weaving and repairing the fabric of society is incalculable. It is a bottom up, not a top down solution.

Over time, however, as we have turned away from the things that actively promote the essential bonds of our traditional relationships, as we have become mired in the process of redefining the basic terms of language and culture, we create our own realities and identities in part as responses to the failure of those relationships. Unable to rely on each other, we turn almost exclusively to government to engineer solutions to the resulting

---

4. Such governmental initiatives are not necessary merely to quell the occasional lapse in judgment by basically good people. They are logistically massive responses to a global problem—systemic evil, or sin.

social ills, solutions designed to pander to our self-interest or identities and maintain power by currying favor and, hence, votes.

Our human nature is to find our identities or fulfillment in our sexuality, appearance, preferences, and those things we can acquire or control (money, power, etc.). For that is how we are, or wish to be, perceived by others. As discussed above, most divisions are functions of our relative self-identities, of how we see ourselves as compared to others. We naturally segregate into groups defined by our preferred identities or goals.

The Christian's identity, however, is not found in his or her body or genetic makeup. Nor is it found in personal desires, preferences, or materialism. Though important, it is not even primarily defined by the fellowship that one Christian shares with another Christian, or the "church." It is an identity found strictly in God's love. The only thing to which a Christian should attempt to compare themselves is the love of Christ. Not the temporal, but the spiritual. The ultimate goal of a Christian has already been reached in their salvation—that gift of special grace. Thereafter, the only goal is to live in the unity of Christ's love. That spiritual love then defines and unites the body of Christ—the church.

Contrarily, the hypersensitive emphasis on self and self-interest drives relative-identity politics, forsaking national unity in the process. We live in a world complicated by self-interest and the abuse of power, by the relative applications or competing definitions of freedom. For the believing Christian, faith provides the ultimate definition of perfect freedom—one by which we measure all others, one based in humility and love. The freedom Christians have in Christ is perfect. It is not dependent on the state of our laws, or government, or this world and its power structures because it exists outside of them.

A government that acknowledges this freedom and allows the people to seek it out and freely express it, as guaranteed in our Constitution, is obviously preferable. But in reality it matters not what the government does, for freedom in Christ exists even in the depths of totalitarianism and other movements home and abroad that actively strive to repress free expression.[5] Our choice, then, is to expend our lives either in safeguarding this truth and hope or in repressing it.

---

5. Christianity has both secular and non-secular foes. Persecution of Christians in the Middle East and Africa by radical Islamists—in Syria, Iran, Iraq, Egypt, and northern Sudan, for example—is particularly brutal, as it is in nonsectarian places such as China and North Korea.

We see this in other cultures where freedom in Christ is much more difficult to express openly. It has also happened in this nation.[6] Even where expression of that freedom is stifled by government—even to the point of death—freedom lives on in the believer, in the kingdom of God in which he or she exists, in eternal life. These are things an imperious government can neither understand nor take away. Such a government merely leverages the fear that this life and the material things it supplies are all there is—get it while you can.

Our founders assured the people of this nation an unobstructed path to attaining and expressing this ultimate freedom. Preserving that freedom acknowledged the power in Christ's example of sacrifice, humility, and love—the true attributes of that city upon a hill. The kingdom of God is that city. And in emulating Christ's love and humility toward others, we too are that city, coming together, sharing those gifts of grace, and welcoming the world to come and join in our freedom. In such a way, this nation was meant to be a model for the entire world.

6. As an example of that repression, during the second term of President Barack Obama (2012–2016), his administration used the power of the Internal Revenue Service to strong-arm and stifle the free expression of certain conservative and/or faith-based organizations by wrongfully withholding applications for tax-exempt status. In late October of 2017, the U.S. Department of Justice announced that the government entered into monetary settlement agreements with the affected groups (more than four hundred of them), with an apology from the IRS.

10

Paul the Apostle and the Road to Freedom

PEOPLE UNIFY IN FAITH, in part, for the purpose of lifting one another up when a broken society and its attendant government fail to inspire and provide hope. First-century Christians were no different. They were hunted down, persecuted, and often killed for seeking shelter in that faith. Today we are guaranteed the freedom to see that faith fulfilled in our lives without interference. Yet despite that freedom, many are still working hard to silence the Christian perspective. Believers suffer the same persecution experienced by the early Christians at the hands of those who see that faith as a threat to their personal or political interests—or as a rebuke to their self-image or individual sovereignty.

Few have done more to advance that freedom, that gift of grace, and the ideals enshrined in that city upon a hill, than the first-century Apostle Paul. Prior to his Christian conversion, however, Paul rabidly persecuted followers of Jesus Christ. As Scripture relates, during the early Christian movement, Stephen, a disciple of Christ, was arrested for blasphemy and brought before the Sanhedrin (a council of elders or rabbis) to answer the charges against him. His defense of the faith angered the crowd. They "dragged him out of the city and began to stone him. Meanwhile, the witnesses laid their clothes at the feet of a young man named Saul."[1] Stephen's last words were, "Lord, do not hold this sin against them."[2] Paul's persecution of Christians began juxtaposed against Stephen's forgiveness of those who were killing him.

Like today's penchant for political correctness, Paul's rigid adherence to religious legalism blinded him to Christ's message of ultimate freedom. He failed to see that God placed the law of the Old Testament before the people in part to make them aware of their sin, as well as establish their utter inability to keep that law regardless of how hard they tried to comply. In foretelling the birth of Christ,[3] God revealed through the Old Testament prophets that our salvation lies not in fulfilling the minutia of the law, nor in continual sacrifice at the altar as atonement for our sins (external human effort), but in the extraordinary life and sacrificial death of the Messiah—the one perfect sacrifice.[4]

No longer was our salvation and, hence, ultimate freedom a matter of mechanically performing rituals and keeping the law, of continually trying but failing to do good. Rather, it was a matter of faith, an understanding that Christ's perfect sacrifice was completely sufficient to reconcile us to God.[5] By accepting this gift, turning away from our sins, and reestablishing that long-lost intimate relationship with our Creator, we could inherit eternal life, equality, freedom—and peace in our relationships with each other.

Paul's conversion and subsequent evangelical ministry began dramatically when the resurrected Christ revealed himself to Paul while he was on his way to Damascus to find and arrest Christians and bring them back to Jerusalem for punishment. Jesus said, "Saul! Saul! Why do you persecute

---

1. Acts 7:58. Saul was Paul's given name. See also Acts 22:20.

2. Acts 7:60.

3. As prophesied by the Old Testament prophet Isaiah, "For to us a child is born, to us a son is given, and the government will be on his shoulders. And he will be called Wonderful Counselor, Mighty God, Everlasting Father, Prince of Peace." (Isa 9:6).

4. "For God so loved the world that he gave his one and only Son, that whoever believes in him shall not perish but have eternal life." (John 3:16).

5. Paul, explaining Christ's complete fulfillment of the law on our behalf, said:

> Therefore, there is now no condemnation for those who are in Christ Jesus, because through Christ Jesus the law of the Spirit who gives life has set you free from the law of sin and death. For what the law was powerless to do because it was weakened by the flesh, God did by sending his own Son in the likeness of sinful flesh to be a sin offering. And so he condemned sin in the flesh, in order that the righteous requirement of the law might be fully met in us, who do not live according to the flesh but according to the Spirit. (Rom 8:1–4)

me?"[6] The terrified man asked, "Who are you, Lord?" The response was, "I am Jesus of Nazareth, whom you are persecuting."[7] On hearing this, Paul was struck blind, and he remained sightless until he reached Damascus. There a man named Ananias revealed to him God's word, at which time his sight was restored.[8]

Paul, a highly learned scholar of Judaic law and tradition (a Pharisee),[9] was already blinded by his rigid adherence to that law. Yet Christ, out of deep love for Paul, restored his sight—literally and spiritually—by *revealing* to him God's truth. He now understood that perfect truth and the true Spirit of the Prime Law. God turned Paul around and placed him on the right path. His zeal for the law was redirected to a zeal for faith. The perfect righteousness he sought was not in the mechanical application of the law, nor in political correctness, nor in his own sense of morality or justice, but in the perfect humility and love of Jesus Christ, *the Spirit behind the Law*—the perfect truth from which our true freedom, equality, and justice are derived.

God's truth emerged. Our God-given freedom and equality had been freed from the control of sinful, subjective, relative human law. In God's forgiveness no longer were we unwilling slaves to the fear and penalty of law, but rather its masters in our understanding and acceptance of the Spirit of love from which the law arose.

God worked through Paul to establish this perfect faith throughout the world. He lived out that reality for the rest of his difficult life. And because of his efforts and the efforts of those like him, we can today claim that reality for ourselves, applying it to all of our relationships, including those comprising our government. His ardent message was that Christ restored

---

6. Acts 22:7 (as related by the Apostle Luke, who is credited with writing the Book of Acts).

7. Acts 22:8.

8. See Acts 22:11–16. Instead of revealing his plan to Paul there on the road to Damascus, Jesus notably sent him to Ananias, who then revealed God's plan for him. At a minimum we can say from this that God uses his people mightily to advance his kingdom. It reveals a truly sublime potential in us all to do God's will, to have his trust. There is no higher honor for a Christian than to have God's trust and faith. He released Paul's potential to help change the world.

9. Paul lists his qualifications in Phil 3:4–6:

> If someone else thinks they have reason to put confidence in flesh, I have more: circumcised on the eighth day, of the people of Israel, of the tribe of Benjamin, a Hebrew of Hebrews; in regard to the law, a Pharisee; as for zeal, persecuting the church; as for righteousness based on the law, faultless.

our relationship with God—and thus with one another—in forgiveness. From that forgiveness comes reconciliation, healed relationships, and unity. Christ embodied the Prime Law.

We do not all have conversions as spectacular as Paul's. But then again, not all of us are asked to live lives of incredible hardship and die for the cause. In fact, all of the original apostles except John were martyred for their faith.[10] Paul's circumstances were unique, and God used them for advantage. Though he was a Jew from the tribe of Benjamin, Paul was also a Roman citizen. Citizenship was a Roman's most valuable and cherished possession; it provided status and rights. While it could be purchased at great cost, Paul was a citizen from birth, born in Tarsus, designated a free city in the province of Cilicia by the Romans. That birthright permitted Paul to take God's message directly to Rome and to Caesar after his arrest in Jerusalem for heresy, imprisonment, and subsequent examination by King Agrippa in Caesarea.[11] Only a Roman citizen could claim the right to appeal to Caesar, which Paul did after refusing to return to Jerusalem for trial.

Thus Paul was brilliantly positioned to use existing legal process to proclaim God's perfect Law in the heart of the pagan Roman Empire. From there, along with the arduous work of all the apostles and disciples throughout the region, that truth ultimately spread to the rest of the world. And there, in Rome, Paul paid for it with his life. His execution was an act of governmental censorship on what it considered a subversive threat—a dangerous truth that exposed Rome's corrupt, sinful heart. That same fear of exposure drives Christian persecution today.

Yet Paul had already died to himself. No longer was he Saul, the self-righteous, self-interested Pharisee, he was Paul, the humble apostle, a servant of the selfless, perfect Christ. He willingly sacrificed himself to advance the cause of true freedom and equality throughout the world—not through violence or deception but through love and truth. He proved that the road to freedom is paved with sacrifice, love, and forgiveness. That was Christ's radical message.

It was a painful lesson he learned years before; an argument, a ministry, forged out of personal experience. No doubt Paul came to understand where the martyred Stephen's forgiveness came from—from God himself, and that he was the direct beneficiary of that forgiveness. As he looked

---

10. Paul was not one of the original twelve apostles.

11. Herod Agrippa II was then King of Judea. After hearing Paul, Agrippa said, "This man could have been set free if he had not appealed to Caesar" (Acts 26:32).

back upon that defining event, the depth of Stephen's love surely cut him like a knife, incising the ignorance and self-interest that fueled Paul's blind persecution of Christ's truth.[12]

Our founders each faced the same decision we do today, to believe in faith or not. Like Paul, we are all blind until we make that critical link between our sin (our imperfection) and God's righteousness (his perfection). Paul experienced that link through his conversion experience on the road to Damascus. He discovered firsthand that we can have an intimate, personal relationship with God without any intercession other than that of Christ himself. His life testified that through that one personal relationship, and the internal flame it sparks, we too can change the world through our relationships with others.

12. See Paul's words in Acts 22:19–20.

11

Perfect Gift v. Relative Entitlement

OUR GOVERNMENT WAS CREATED in part by individuals who, like Paul, understood God's gift of eternal life and its effect on the way we relate to one another. Arguably, the greatest contribution Reformed[1] Christianity supplies to our democracy is its emphasis on the doctrine of salvation by faith alone and rejection of "works justification," the misleading idea, mentioned above, that an individual can earn God's favor—and hence salvation—by performing good deeds or simply by being a good person (whatever "good"

1. The term is used here to refer to that which arose as a product of the Protestant Reformation, from Martin Luther's revelation after studying the New Testament, particularly the writings of Paul, that people are justified (made right with God) by faith alone through God's grace, not by self-effort or the intercession of others. His concerns about the Catholic Church's doctrines were submitted in his famous 1517 written protest, *The Ninety-Five Theses*. Luther's motivation was in part to expose the hypocrisy of the church selling dispensations or indulgences for the forgiveness of sins to individuals who could pay for it. This seems justifiable if salvation is a function of our own efforts. The payment itself could be justified as a good work. Luther's efforts earned him excommunication from the church by Pope Leo X. Sixty years or so earlier, Johann Gutenberg's press produced the first book ever printed using movable type—the Holy Bible—which opened the door to bringing the unfiltered Word of God directly to the people. This would ultimately free the Christian faith from those in power who, up until that time, controlled the Word of God, manipulating it for their own ends in the name of the church. Luther had the audacity to translate Scripture from Latin into vernacular German so it could be readily understood. His work held up truth to power, revealing the influence of self-interest on obscuring that truth.

really means). Rather, salvation is a gift of God's perfect grace. We can accept it only by faith. It is neither earned nor deserved.

Because of our inherent imperfection, any act we might conduct on our own to earn salvation is undermined by that sin and thus utterly inadequate. It is therefore commonly said that we are saved *for* good works, not *by* them.[2] We do good things, not to earn God's love, but rather because God already loves us and we desire to pass on that love to others. In serving others, we return to God the love he has so freely given us. Contrarily, when salvation is deemed conditional or relative, we are free to devise whatever means we desire to accomplish this goal. In the extreme, mandating specific acts as prerequisites to obtaining faith's ultimate goal potentially opens the door to radicalization, for example, in the act of self-martyrdom or the application of terror.

Those with apparent power or authority use prerequisites to press conformance in others. Hence, the radical can say to the moderate, "You have not dyed your hair green—you are not doing enough for the cause. You are weak in the faith, and you will be punished. Nonbelievers must die!" The moderate rejects this as morally repugnant because life—a gift from a merciful God—seems worth preserving. But the individual is reluctant to question or rein in the radical due to the prospect of being shunned or punished for noncompliance. Yet the Christian doctrine of salvation provides that accepting Christ into one's life is an act of faith. Only *after* receiving that gift can the individual then begin to understand God's hand in drawing him or her to himself, as well as the influence of past life events on ultimately having responded to that call.

Intellectual reason cannot grasp this purely spiritual event. It is completely personal and unique. It is meant to be. In that salvation, and the spiritual growth that follows, an individual's purpose is revealed. That purpose, a response to God's call upon one's life, cannot be compelled by anyone. No individual, church, or government can prevent God's perfect work in an individual and thus change the outcome. Indoctrination of any kind is simply a form of works justification which the true Christian faith wholly rejects. *No one* can force another to love God or his Word. Those

---

2. This summarizes the Apostle Paul's original statement in Eph 2:8–10, which provides:

> For it is by grace you have been saved, through faith—and this is not from yourselves, it is the gift of God—not by works, so that no one can boast. For we are God's handiwork, created in Christ Jesus to do good works, which God prepared in advance for us to do.

who try only pervert the faith for their own selfish ends. True Christianity demands absolutely nothing from those who do not believe. It never compels or berates. It merely invites examination of a better way.

The moderate's reticence, however, is like that experienced by the rank and file under authoritarian/totalitarian movements. In such radical faiths or regimes, the core element is not love but fear—the fear of rejection, deprivation, physical punishment, or death. Accountability is not the willing desire to return God's love for the sake of others, but rather a reaction compelled by failure and the fear of alienation or punishment—from either imperious adherents or an imperious god.[3] That difference is at the very core of the freedom our founders provided in our unique democracy—the difference between freedom in love and slavery in fear.

The threat of penalty is not what keeps the Christian from sinning or breaking the law. It is the knowledge that the penalty for those sins has already been paid, and to continue to sin is to ignore and undermine the unimaginable price and humility of that sacrifice—all for our forgiveness. It dishonors God. In honoring that ultimate love, we are aided by the Spirit in our efforts to maintain our faith in God—just as honoring the sacrifice of our patriots keeps us from losing faith in our nation.

Freedom in love is at the very center of the relationship between the Christian faith and our democracy. God's gift of salvation was memorialized in our Declaration of Independence when Thomas Jefferson, hoping for new life in that freedom, declared that we are all *endowed* by our Creator with inalienable rights, among which are life, liberty, and the pursuit of happiness. An endowment is a gift, neither merited nor deserved, flowing generously from one individual to another. Our inalienable rights are endowments from God, perfect gifts of his perfect grace. When we secularize those rights, removing God as their source, they become relative entitlements. Now out of God's hands, anything can be justified. What one person creates another can simply change or take away.

The ultimate struggle between freedom in love and slavery in fear is manifested in the manipulation of our rights, where they are measured not by what we already have (the positive), but rather by what we do not have (the negative); not by what they are, but by what we subjectively want them to be in order to suit our self-interests or images. We are no longer

---

3. For example, the brutal murders and enslavement by the extreme radical Islamic State of Iraq and Syria (ISIS) of infidel Muslims and Christians alike, allegedly for the faith, thereby compelling compliance to its destructive ideals.

thankful for the gift. We are instead envious of those who, compared to ourselves, appear entitled or have something we do not. We desire—in fact, demand—the same blessings for ourselves.

While we are free to make demands upon government, we are not, however, free to make demands upon God. We need someone other than ourselves to whom we can shift—or from whom we can demand—accountability. Yet we cannot demand a gift. It must be freely given and freely accepted. A gift is solely the function of the donor's intent, not the donee's demand. Nor, unless offered, may one rightfully demand that the donor alter the nature of the gift to suit the recipient's desires. It can only be accepted as is or rejected outright. Otherwise it is not a true gift.

Our *demand* for the gift is the genesis of our nation's entitlement mentality. We rely solely on the government to supply those rights we demand, and in so doing we substitute slavery to the bureaucracy for the freedom that is already ours in God's perfect gift. The Christian founders understood that while those rights are intrinsic to our humanity, they originate in God as creator. Our freedom comes from God, not man.

The divine origin of our human freedom and equality was the basis for rejecting the class distinctions inherent in the British aristocracy. Real equality and freedom, and the democracy flowing therefrom, were not birthrights of the privileged, those who could pay for it (much like those buying freedom (dispensations) from the church for their sins), but the birthright of us all as children of God. It is in the realization of this natural birthright that we appreciate the virtue of limited central government—the distribution of power among free and equal people. By propagating the fallacy that those God-given rights are man-made entitlements, we stoke the progressive need for a large central bureaucracy for the administration of those entitlements. This need caused progressives like Karl Marx, communism's progenitor, to famously disparage religion as the people's opiate, a numbing crutch, despite the truth that faith put real power not in government, but in the people.

However, self-justification is not limited to tyrants. Many individuals, even many nominal Christians, see salvation as a function of good intent, of simply carrying out those deeds they perceive as good. They see the value of the biblical moral imperative of goodness, but do not fully understand that true Christian morality is an all-or-nothing response. The relative sentiment that "all roads lead to God" creates disagreement about who God is, and what constitutes core Christianity, morality, and the nature of the freedom the faith provides. In the process of choosing those things we feel suffice in reaching faith's ultimate goal, we each create the god of our own imperfect personal desires.[4] In so doing, we ourselves become that god, rendering our inalienable rights mere relative entitlements to be defined and redefined as often as we like. Therein we perfect our self-images, our idolatry, our sin.

Even so, the physical manifestation of that sin is not the primary concern, but rather the state of the heart which permits the sin to become manifest. A change of heart is the critical imperative, in which case the sinful act would be less likely to take place.[5] Attributing our good works to ourselves as a sole function of our own altruism or intent, rather than to God working through us as a result of our faith, inevitably results in the divisive need to compare ourselves—our goodness—to others. We elevate our self-motivation and image rather than the cooperative Spirit of God who gave us the will to do it.[6]

As a result of Christ's perfect, selfless sacrifice, the Christian faith is immune to denigration. Anyone can disparage God, mock Jesus, burn Bibles, tear down crosses, shake fists, rant, rave, yell, call people infidels or haters, or even blow oneself or others up. In terms of salvation it simply does not matter. If a person has received the gift of salvation, he or she has reached—in this life—faith's ultimate goal. And it can never be taken away.

While we continue to struggle with the battles of each day, the war is already won. This is not to say that we cannot protect ourselves and others against violence. We have the gift of our God-given right to life and liberty, which should not be relative. Many heroes sacrificed themselves so that

---

4. In a teaching moment Jesus Christ said, "Thus, by their fruit you will recognize them. Not everyone who says to me, 'Lord, Lord,' will enter the kingdom of heaven, but only the one who does the will of my Father who is in heaven." (Matt 7:20–21). The will of God is our obedience to his Word, not simply to our own sense of that which seems right or just.

5. See, e.g., 1 John 3:15: "Anyone who hates a brother or sister is a murderer." The Apostle John's point is that the act of murder is only the manifestation of a hateful heart. Likewise, Jesus said, "Anyone who looks at a woman lustfully has already committed adultery with her in his heart." (Matt 5:28).

6. See Matt 6:1, 3–4:

> Be careful not to practice your righteousness in front of others to be seen by them. If you do, you will have no reward from your Father in heaven. . . . But when you give to the needy, do not let your left hand know what your right hand is doing, so that your giving may be in secret. Then your Father, who sees what is done in secret, will reward you.

this nation and its ideals might live on. They serve as individual examples of Christ's sacrifice for us all.

But we are not to use that faith as sole justification for taking a life. God's perfect Word is capable of defending itself. We are free to assert its wisdom as shining the light on a better way and, particularly, on our own faults. But to kill another merely for the sake of unbelief is a violation of God's sixth commandment—"You shall not murder."[7] To dub ourselves the arm of God's ultimate spiritual justice is pure vanity, an act of entitlement, an abuse of the perfect gift.[8]

---

7. Exod 20:13.

8. Lest we forget, recall the January 7, 2015, attack by radical Islamists against the Paris-based magazine *Charlie Hebdo*, killing twelve for publishing satirical cartoons of Muhammad. Or the horrendous November 13, 2015, attacks in Paris that killed 130 people. Or the forty-nine dead and fifty-three wounded in the Orlando, Florida, nightclub shooting of June 12, 2016. Or the shooting of twenty hostages taken by Islamists in Dhaka, Bangladesh, on July 1, 2016. Or the car bombing that killed more than 140 people in Baghdad, Iraq, on July 3, 2016. Or the July 14, 2016, truck attack on Bastille Day celebrations in Nice, France, killing eighty-four. Or ISIS's horrific practices of beheadings, burnings, and torture of innocents at the hand of those claiming to do the will of Allah.

12

A More Perfect Union
The Individual v. The State

CHRISTIANITY IS A FAITH system that, like our democracy, provides the mechanism for forming a more perfect union—between ourselves and God, and thus with each other. It is a unity that in our sin we could never achieve on our own. The order inherent in the difference between God's perfection and our imperfection informs our respect for God's Prime Law as being the superior foundation for our secular law. Real democracy is born in the recognition of that order. God has, in that spiritual Prime Law, provided us with our ultimate freedom and equality. And just like our salvation, nothing can alter or take away a freedom or equality that has a spiritual origin.

How we apply this truth to our lives and to our democracy was revealed to us in the life of Christ, in his humility before God, and his creations, as evidenced by his willing submission—the ultimate mark of personal accountability. This is the connecting thread running through the Old and New Testaments of the Bible: that imperfect people can never fully comply with the perfect law given to them by a perfect God.

No amount of sacrifice, ritual, blind obedience, or zealousness could ever suffice for the purpose of reaching faith's ultimate goal of salvation. Those who lived solely by this law, without sincerely embracing its overarching concerns for selfless love, humility, mercy, forgiveness, and justice, would, by their own choice, be enslaved and ultimately judged by this law—a losing proposition since no one could ever comply. In so doing, they merely elevate the outward appearance or form of righteousness over the substance of the faith.

This is the reason God said that it was not empty sacrifice (ritual) that he desires but rather mercy.[1] Sacrificing ourselves for others is itself a sacrifice to God, a means of extending God's mercy to them. It is the fulfillment of the second part of God's Prime Law—to love others. True mercy cannot be understood, let alone dispensed, by someone who has never received it. For if one has never received mercy or forgiveness, they have none to give. The person with a regenerated heart has received that mercy. "Works" in the absence of that mercy, that changed heart, like self-martyrdom, is therefore a meaningless sacrifice, because it comes from a different place, a place of self-righteousness. It is important, then, that we consider our motivations for the sacrifices we make. Are they made mercifully for others, or solely for ourselves or our personal or political agendas?

Because God's standard is absolute perfection, it is pointless to say, "We're cutting off heads and blowing ourselves up all day long, and that should be enough." It is not. And it never will be—because God's perfect standard is *not* relative. We insist on measuring God's perfect standard by our own imperfect standards, demanding that an omnipotent God stand before us and explain himself, to conform to our fallible sense of justice and propriety. In our utter inability to keep it, we curse that standard, and God, as being terribly unfair.

Yet we miss the point entirely. Those who live by faith will never be judged by that law. Having already been forgiven, in God's infinite mercy, for their inability to keep it, they have been freed from its ultimate punishment—spiritual death. The faithful have been made perfectly righteous in God's eyes, not by anything they have done or could do, but by Christ's atoning sacrifice. Not because they are worthy, but because *he* is worthy.

In feathering our nests and padding our spiritual resumes, we overlook this truth. Proactively killing ourselves or others for the sake of the faith is the ultimate in empty, vain gestures. The believer has received God's mercy. Having understood and accepted its cost, the believer is changed fundamentally—an approved and willing conduit for passing on that mercy and love to others. Not by judging others, but by example—inviting comparison not to one's imperfect self, but rather to God's perfect love.

Christians are often accused of being judgmental. Those who fail to grasp the significance of their own sin and forgiveness most certainly are.

---

1. See Hos 6:6. See also Matt 9:13.

It is not a Christian's prerogative to judge the state of another's heart—particularly those of non-Christians. We can only empathize with another's conduct as reflecting the state of our own heart. To judge another is to enter a realm reserved for God himself—and we foolishly do so at our own peril.[2] Christ came to us to establish the preeminence of God's perfect Law, to teach by example, not to judge.[3] True compliance does not come from fear of that perfect Law, or fear of punishment, but rather from love of the Law.[4] In that love we are no longer a slave to the Law, but free as its master.

We too are a government of myriad laws and regulations that, on our own, we can never perfectly keep no matter how hard we try. So how do we best come together corporately, as a union, for the purpose of governing ourselves? Our submission in faith—that love of God's higher Law—enables us to better craft and comply with our secular laws, to live more righteous, moral lives. The attractiveness of that righteous life draws others to desire the same for themselves. That example is the road to unity and peace, a practical connection between the Christian faith and our democracy.

Our ability to voluntarily lead outwardly moral lives is at the heart of that city upon a hill, an example to the rest of the world that this nation, in the spirit of humility, has found favor in God's eyes. In this nation all things are possible because we have received the peace and freedom that only God can provide. His freedom allows us to be the unique individuals God created us to be. The Apostle Paul reminded the Corinthians, "Now the Lord is the Spirit, and where the Spirit of the Lord is, there is freedom."[5] Does the Spirit reside in us individually and corporately?[6] In the absence of that Spirit, are we truly free?[7]

2. "Do not judge, or you too will be judged. For in the same way you judge others, you will be judged, and with the measure you use, it will be measured to you." (Matt 7:1–2).

3. "If anyone hears my words but does not keep them, I do not judge that person. For I did not come to judge the world, but to save the world." (John 12:47).

4. "Whoever looks intently into the perfect law that gives freedom, and continues in it—not forgetting what they have heard, but doing it—they will be blessed in what they do." (Jas 1:25).

5. 2 Cor 3:17.

6. "And you also were included in Christ when you heard the message of truth, the gospel of your salvation. When you believed, you were marked in him with a seal, the promised Holy Spirit." (Eph 1:13).

7. The Apostle Paul likewise counseled the Galatians on the freedom they have in the Sprit:

You, my brothers and sisters, were called to be free. But do not use your freedom

Mindful of human nature, our founders wisely foreclosed any governmental power to either pre- or proscribe a particular form of religious practice. As regards faith, the best government can do is foster the individual's quest for truth—even if that quest does not include considering the path offered by Jesus Christ. That is what the First Amendment to the Constitution guarantees: to follow the dictates of one's heart, to think as one wishes to think.

For the believing Christian, a government that would, by law or any other means, attempt to coerce a person into accepting God or a particular mode of belief belies a true understanding of the Christian God. Only a deep understanding and acceptance of the moral imperative Christianity supplies through God's wisdom and virtue matters. This is something no government can provide or force upon an individual.

Therefore, the issue is not what the government can impose upon individuals by way of religion, but rather what individuals, in their faith, impart to the relationships that comprise their government. The believing Christian would never rightfully assume that an omnipotent God needs any one of us to establish a government for the purpose of promoting his agenda. The Christian quest for God is neither external nor corporate. It is profoundly internal and personal. The nature of the quest makes it so. The Christian framers of our nation's Constitution understood that it is not government's place to interfere in God's uniquely personal work within the individual, where the most crucial debate is the one we have inside ourselves—the primary battle site of the war for eternal freedom.

Examples abound of politicians or other public figures making broad public statements about the need for policy reflecting the "Christian" thing—the implication being that if you do not agree with that policy or the means they proffer to carry it out, you must be unchristian. It is a form of shame politics, a better-than-thou hypocrisy that speaks for itself. Such pronouncements reveal the speaker's fundamental ignorance of the faith: that being a good Christian is, on balance, simply appearing to do more good than bad, rather than whole-hearted obedience in faith. Or worse,

---

to indulge the flesh; rather, serve one another humbly in love. For the entire law is fulfilled in keeping this one command: "Love your neighbor as yourself." If you bite and devour each other, watch out or you will be destroyed by each other.

So I say, walk by the Spirit, and you will not gratify the desires of the flesh [sinful nature]. For the flesh desires what is contrary to the Spirit, and the Spirit what is contrary to the flesh. They are in conflict with each other, so that you are not to do whatever you want. (Gal 5:13–17)

that we should, in judgment of others, subject them to that vision. At best it confuses subjective humanity with Christianity's objective humility, revealing an indifference to the truth for the sake of the individual's personal or political agenda.

The path to a more perfect understanding is part of the individual's journey in faith, a journey that government may support, but never join. Some have suggested that the form of government that best expresses our corporate Christian values is socialism or communism in their perceived humanity—that Jesus, in essence, was a socialist—manipulating Christ and God's kingdom for base political advantage. This is ironic in that the main progenitors of those secular economic philosophies abhorred faith altogether. They saw peace and happiness as a function of economic policy—of the equal distribution of "wealth/things"—itself an admission that our nature is ruled by self-interest and materialism. Faith was simply a delusion.

SOCIALISM/COMMUNISM V. CAPITALISM—A BASIC OVERVIEW

It is often said that money is the root of all evil. But money, as a means of exchange, is a useful and necessary tool. It is more truthful to say that the root of evil is the heart that abuses or misuses that tool. We find security in wealth. It provides our basic needs. It shields us from hardship and uncertainty. Unfortunately, imperfect individuals can take that need for security to great extremes. That fear of want most assuredly affects secular public policy. What interferes most in secular government is in fact a root disagreement on economics—how to control wealth or its production and the security it provides.

Whereas communism and/or socialism are basically *social/economic theories* that dictate both political and economic structure and control, democracy is a *political theory* in which market-driven capitalism is derivative, arising out of our democratic freedom to live and work as we wish. Capitalism, as an economic theory, does not itself dictate political structure.[8] The battle between these two ideologies has contributed greatly to the disunity in this world as they compete for dominance.

---

8. This is not to say that money does not influence democratic politics. It most certainly does, for good *and* bad. Much of government entails how revenues are to be collected and spent—a process rife with opportunity for adulteration by self-interest. Any lobbyist can attest to that. Just as money would influence a church to sell dispensations

ECONOMIC EQUITY V. EQUALITY OF ECONOMIC OPPORTUNITY

Communism/socialism generally holds that government should supply, or at least endeavor to supply, actual *economic equity*, where no one has more wealth or goods than another. In order to provide that parity, there must be an extremely large centralized bureaucracy—a powerful federal government owning and/or controlling property and the means of production, thereby controlling economic policy and the flow of money.[9]

Capitalism, on the other hand, holds that it is government's limited responsibility to help provide, as with all individual freedoms, equality of *economic opportunity*. Government should promote freedom of equal opportunity, leaving market forces and risk to determine success and failure. Individuals, or groups of individuals, risk investing their personal capital, hoping to be rewarded by a return on that investment—i.e., risk and reward. That willingness to accept personal risk (or accountability) helps drive efficiency, creativity, and innovation. That risk is minimized by diligence and hard work. The cost of labor is a factor of that risk and reward.

Capitalist and communist views on labor are distinguishing features. Labor in capitalism is viewed primarily as an exchange of service for pay—a

---

for salvation to those who could afford it, the government likewise sells access or influence in the political process for personal or private interests.

9. The most obvious recent example of social/economic reform was the Affordable Care Act of 2010, or "Obamacare," a forced industry evolution into a single-payer, government-run medical system—a socialist program similar to those found in many countries around the world. Generally, it mandated that all individuals who could not afford private plans must buy into health plans sponsored and controlled by the government, or pay a penalty. That penalty was upheld by the Supreme Court in a 2012 5–4 decision as legitimate means of taxation. During the Trump administration Congress repealed the mandate in 2017, rendering the purchase of the insurance voluntary, not mandatory. Spending on health care amounts to about one-fifth of this nation's Gross Domestic Product—a huge sum. Socialism is about transferring wealth from the producers to the consumers (as represented by the government). Hence, President Obama effected a massive shift of power and wealth in this nation at the cost of individual freedom. Liberals justify this by exclaiming that health care is a right. Even if true, it does not follow that government *must* provide it. It should protect our right to acquire it, but not dictate what, when, where, or how it is acquired. The Second Amendment, for example, guarantees our right to acquire firearms for our personal protection—much the same reason we acquire insurance. But that does not mean that government must supply them—nor should it. There is a vast difference between reasonable regulation to ensure that right, and the usurpation of an entire industry ultimately interfering with the fundamental nature of the right.

quid pro quo. While there are exceptions, the laborer typically has no direct ownership interest in the means of its production. This perceived economic/monetary or class inequity between ownership and labor is the "evil" communism seeks to correct by giving each laborer a cooperative ownership interest in the product in which they have contributed their labor, and the means by which it is produced.

Ownership entails risk. The capitalist risks losing their investment. Creditors risk losing monies lent to the owner. When the business fails, labor suffers as well—jobs are lost. While this risk of loss provides motivation to succeed, in some instances it, admittedly, does not always work.[10] However, success in communism is not measured by a personal return on investment. It is ideally measured by the well-being of the State. If the State is well, the people are collectively well. Capital for the business is supplied by the State. Profits (if any) from the business belong to the State. The State is one massive business enterprise comprised of State-run corporations (i.e., "State Capitalism"). Risk of loss is minimized by the backing of the State's considerable resources, which, in turn, should ideally support job security as those resources are equitably redistributed. The backing of the weighty State treasury has the added global advantage of reducing competition and, thus, free enterprise, thereby strengthening the State.

Ideals, however, always succumb to practical application. First conjured in secular elite intellectual circles—the *Intelligentsia*—both Chinese and Russian communism leveraged worker distress: Lenin, the industrial worker, and Mao, the rural agricultural peasant. The pure Marxist ideals of Vladimir Lenin's 1917 Russian Revolution influenced Mao Zedong to form the Chinese Communist party in 1921—and led to the Chinese Revolution of 1949. But to differing degrees, the failure of those revolutionary socialist ideals/economies to sufficiently supply the needs of the people led to certain capitalist free market reforms in each. They compromised by injecting into the system a dose of the evil ideology they abhorred—a modicum of personal control/ownership, the very basis of class distinctions. Entrepreneurship developed in each system allowing individuals to become wealthy and powerful, if not corrupt, in the process—today's oligarchs. The wealthy classes which communism sought to erase, stubbornly live on.

The individual's overwhelming desire for freedom of thought and a personal stake in the outcome in their life, however, reveals the Achilles heel of both Chinese and Soviet systems—the failure of communism/

---

10. Hence the advent of bankruptcy laws, a safety net for failed businesses.

socialism to supply what the individual really needed most, not just physically to survive, but emotionally to feel personally fulfilled. Dictating parity by force of law encroaches upon our individual freedom to live and work as we wish—to satisfy that deep emotional need. As does forcing individuals to subscribe to the political party that supports that ideal—which is what the hardline ruling Communist parties did. It is what all tyrants do. Unlike dutiful ants all working blindly for the collective survival of the colony, humans have an individual will and desire for freedom that must be expressed.

Generally, progressives feel that many people cannot avail themselves of that opportunity because of their social conditions—conditions created by those with wealth, hence the emphasis on the socialist ideal of universal income equality—as reflected in the desire for *external* global social change. (Unlike capitalism's forward-looking risk and reward, it is an ideology based in victimhood and reparation—a rear-view system designed to fix a "problem.")

Yet that same rear-view demand for external change has spawned the movements of identity politics and political correctness and the environment of blame in which they thrive—what is today the woke or cancel culture—and the need to deny history and convention. The authoritarian demand that we subscribe to another's self-image or identity is exactly the same as demanding membership in the political party that supports that identity or ideal. Our inability or refusal to first seek an internal solution drives the demand for an external solution—a demand for change in others, the demand for conformance. In China and Russia the communist answer was an external State solution. Disunity arises when others inevitably refuse that external demand to change—to knuckle under.

Conservatives, on the other hand, feel that regardless of social condition, opportunity is created and driven by an individual's will and desire for self-improvement, hence the emphasis on internal change, self-effort, perseverance, and accountability. Government simply needs to get out of the way and let it happen.

There is no doubt that individual success can bring out one's blindness or insensitivity to the socio-economic disadvantage of others—or the abuse of one's wealth. Our lack of humility has contributed significantly to social and economic disparities. Taking advantage of others is, in *all* events, sinful, evidencing the need for greater humility—a theme of this essay. For the Christian this is where their faith intervenes. But there is no demand that others change, because to do so is to interfere with another's freedom and, potentially, with God's plan for their lives (i.e., that unique personal experience God uses on their path back to him).

The freedom we all have to compete economically frees us from the slavery of forced economic equality—a manufactured equality requiring increased governmental intervention through the proliferation of law and regulation, and a larger, more powerful government. It is the freedom to think for ourselves in *all* things: our vocations, education, art, or anything else. For the quality of our lives should, to the greatest extent possible, be determined by the decisions that we freely make for ourselves, not those made for us by others.

Marxism proposes that once people are free from economic competition, they will be free to pursue and develop their unique individual intellectual and artistic differences—higher human endeavors, its vision for a more perfect individual and, thus, a more perfect society. Unfortunately, that dream comes with a serious cost as government, by law or regulation, hypocritically reaches into and controls the means by which those differences are developed, i.e., thought and expression, in order to prevent free criticism of that "ideal" society. Free thought fosters critical thinking and expression. The contradiction is obvious: free thought must first be accountable to the political and social agenda (political correctness).[11] There is no independence from the "State." The individual and State are one. The individual is forced to accept the State as his or her identity or image.

Maintaining that economic intervention ultimately requires the need to control individual thought and action—the suppression of our human will—to counter our natural desire to be free in all things. That is indoctrination. And it is not difficult to see the seeds of that indoctrination in our nation's current pernicious trend to censor free speech[12] and influence

11. This is already happening here in the U.S. In 2020, the Academy of Motion Picture Arts and Sciences announced standards for representation and inclusion in films in order to be eligible for its best picture award, "designed to encourage equitable representation on and off screen in order to better reflect the diversity of the movie-going audience." Accessed at https://www.oscars.org/news/academy-establishes-representation-and-inclusion-standards-oscarsr-eligibility. Both art and artist (here film and film maker) must be accountable to the social and political views of those for whom the art is being produced, at least for those artists desiring that particular accolade and the money it generates.

12. For example, powerful tech companies like Google® control a large portion of internet access and, potentially, the information disseminated through it. The power to restrict free expression by denying access thereto resides in the company's administrators. Recently, Google administrators, at the behest of NBC, temporarily closed down

global fiscal policy.[13] The end result is the centralized administration/control of law and power wrested from a diverse, free people.

Thus communism attempts to control sinful human nature corporately by forcing equality through centralized secular economic and social means. For its adherents, history proved the ineffectiveness of faith as a moderating factor. God, if he existed at all, never prevented the rich from subjugating the poor. He never stood in the breach to physically intervene in our greed or inhumanity toward others.[14] So the government becomes one's god, one's hope—hope that it will continue to subsidize one's life to its end. Yet if we willingly cede ourselves to the external control of the government, that subsidy, we become slaves to it, to the siren's call of the goods and services it provides—to the things that sustain us.

---

access to the public comments section of *The Federalist*, a conservative media outlet accessible through Google, claiming that the language of its users violated the company's derogatory speech policies. Moreover, Google's actions in stifling expression directly affects the income sources of outlets like *The Federalist* by manipulating its advertisers to abandon it as a marketing platform for fear of bad publicity. See Justice, "A Recap of NBC's Failed Attempt to Deplatform *The Federalist*," accessed at https://thefederalist.com/2020/06/22/a-recap-of-nbcs-failed-attempt-to-deplatform-the-federalist-on-google/. The government has threatened to step in and amend existing law that shields companies like Google from liability for such actions. Whether censorship of free speech or coercive business tactics, neither issue has much good to say about our corporate culture and the individuals controlling it.

13. For what appears as the indoctrination of a socialist or "green" agenda in global finance, consider the 2006 United Nations initiative, ESG (short for Environmental, Social, and Governance), compelling certain moral parameters into the decision-making process behind global investment and finance. The movement is administered by London-based PRI (Principles for Responsible Investment). (See PRI's "About Us" page at https://www.unpri.org/about-us/what-are-the-principles-for-responsible-investment.) Signatories are required to report annually on their ESG initiatives. Notably, among its signatories are several New York State and local government and teacher's union pension funds, including TIAA–CREF (a provider of financial services to academia and government), whose influence might account in part for President Biden's March 2023 veto of a bipartisan bill banning the application of ESG principles in retirement investments, claiming that ESG principles would protect retirement savings. Not everyone participating in those plans are aware that their funds are being invested not to maximize their returns, but rather to fund a shift in corporate social culture, thereby causing the investors to unwittingly support moral/political/social agendas with which they might not agree. And if they are employer sponsored/mandated plans, employees may have no other choice but to comply (therein distinguishing between democratic and socialist conceptions of freedom).

14. For the Christian this is exactly what Christ did on earth—stood in the breach between heaven and hell.

That is not freedom. That is the real opiate of the masses. The addict must repeatedly return to the dealer (the State). The cost of a continuous supply of the drug is a vote (and all the cash we can muster in the form of taxes)—while it lasts. Thus, the class distinctions that Marxism tried so desperately to erase through the redistribution of wealth is really a heart problem—an acknowledgment of the truth that we are all primarily self-interested. But in the absence of compulsory retraining (indoctrination), the purposeful manipulation of economic policy does not remedy that issue. Thus indoctrination is the religion of communism.

For the same sin that infects the recipients of government's largesse— the people—likewise infects those whose job it is to administer that system. It is the exact same sin that causes both capitalist and communist entrepreneurs to abuse their opportunity and wealth. It is the exact same sin that causes the administrators of faith to abuse the faith, or educators their duty of trust. To suggest that those in government operate under a higher, disinterested generosity, or are better educated, wiser, and thus immune to or otherwise above that influence, is completely disingenuous.

The benevolence of government is a monumental lie. Unspoken, of course, but in their hubris that is exactly what many of those administrators, by their very actions, believe: the masses are simply incapable of caring or deciding for themselves. So when sinful people are staring at empty shelves or standing in endless lines waiting for hand-outs from an equally sinful system, we must ask who is really free. That is the ultimate legacy of the elite intelligentsia, the same arrogance at the heart of this nation's liberal socialist politics.

In 1991 the Soviet model of communism crumbled as the all federated satellite states comprising the USSR began declaring their independence. Soviet economic reforms failed. The corruption that overtook the system by individuals who had the power to influence government and markets proved the tenacity of self-interest and inequality. Those who look to the Chinese model as the better alternative only fool themselves. It thrives because it has hypocritically co-opted just enough of our democracy's economic free enterprise to make those in power extremely wealthy, while politically maintaining an iron boot on the human rights of the rank and file.

It is not without some irony that second only to Japan, China has acquired the highest percentage of our nation's debt to foreign nations.[15]

15. See US Treasury, "Major Foreign Holders of Treasury Securities," accessed at https://ticdata.treasury.gov/Publish/mfh.txt.

Such an imposing burden is this debt that it arguably renders this country's remonstration against China's human rights violations mere lip service. The "business" of government undermines the world's perception of our nation's legitimacy as a moral world leader—and rightly so. We have done this to ourselves, consuming more than we produce, living to deficit spend. We refuse personal accountability. This is the example our government provides to our youth and to the world. Slavery is the way it is, so just accept it—get with the program or be left behind.

Yet in faith our indomitable spirit of self-assurance and self-reliance, tempered by love and humility, is God's Spirit exemplified. That Spirit has given us the wisdom and strength to live righteous lives—in freedom—without governmental interference, without the need for "Big Brother" or the political elite to ensure compliance. In faith we value self-control, fairness, veracity, and accountability above power and influence—things we gladly cede to a loving God, a perfect Sovereign who will never abuse that power.

This Spirit is the basis for our unique individualism as expressed collectively in our national exceptionalism, born not from hubris but from love.[16] Our national exceptionalism is sourced in God's grace. It is based in his gifts of life, liberty, and the pursuit of happiness, which we use to do exceptional things. We are compelled to share those things, in the Spirit of love, with others.

16. National exceptionalism has no place in the progressive ideal of a unified global community, where the ultimate prize is a homogenous one-world government. There, individuality has no real value. It is swallowed up in political correctness—in the need to appease and assimilate. National exceptionalism is measured only by what it materially supplies to that process until the goal is reached. After that it is expendable. This is no measure of the unifying Spirit of God within a nation's people. Therein we can understand the utility of the progressive's assertion that this country has never been great—i.e., history with a perpetual asterisk.

13

A House Divided

THAT WILLINGNESS TO SHARE—to submit in our relationships with one another—allows us to form a more perfect union, one born in humility and expressed in perfect equality. Whether they could completely foresee it or not, our founders did something truly extraordinary. They achieved a government like no other, one recognizing the seminal importance of this essential truth as a sustaining principle: the government is subordinate to its people, who are themselves subordinate to an omni-perfect God and perfect Law. We are one free people and, together, one free nation under God. To those who hold this perfect truth in their hearts, and to the government of God that is the ideal, it is the "more perfect" expression of selflessness and equality.

In attributing our equality and rights to the Creator, our founders were recognizing and integrating the importance of faith—and the Spirit infusing it—as that necessary moderating influence upon the general will so that we might have the best chance of addressing the one thing that contributes most to the failure of individuals or the governments they form: self-interest, an interest not sufficiently addressed within the confines of the social contract. They attempted to express and preserve the Spirit of God within the people. That very Spirit allowed us, as a nation, to overcome our dependency on slavery. The same Spirit allows us to continuously overcome our sin.

Perhaps nowhere was the value of sacrifice more eloquently expressed than during the Civil War, in the words of Abraham Lincoln's Gettysburg Address, which provided in part:

> We have come to dedicate a portion of that field as a final resting place for those who here gave their lives that that nation might live. It is altogether fitting and proper that we should do this. But in a larger sense we cannot dedicate, we cannot consecrate, we cannot hallow this ground. The brave men, living and dead, who struggled here have consecrated it, far above our poor power to add or detract. The world will little note, nor long remember, what we say here, but it can never forget what they did here. It is for us the living, rather, to be dedicated here to the unfinished work which they who fought here have thus far so nobly advanced. It is rather for us to be here dedicated to the great task remaining before us, *that from these honored dead we take increased devotion to that cause for which they gave the last full measure of devotion, that we here highly resolve that these dead shall not have died in vain, that this nation, under God, shall have a new birth of freedom, and that government of the people, by the people, for the people, shall not perish from the earth.*[1]

President Lincoln saw a new birth in freedom, made possible by the devotion of those who gave their lives for it. The endurance of our freedom is a function of our devotion to maintaining it. Every individual who, in their faith, has experienced his or her own rebirth in Christ, who has received their freedom under God, understands perfectly this devotion.

Our government was formed in part on our Christian ancestors' devotion to the truth that Jesus loved them so much that he died to free them from the bondage of their sins. No doubt this utterly selfless act emboldened many of them to give their own lives for this country. Many did for the cause of ending slavery. They willingly died for the truth that freedom and equality are gifts from God, and that within that freedom all life is sacred and has value because we are all created in "the image of God."[2]

The freedom envisioned by our founders in the establishment of our democratic way of life is the very image of the archetypal freedom envisioned within God's gift of eternal life to those who believe in him. When

1. Lincoln, "The Gettysburg Address," (emphasis added), accessed at https://tile.loc.gov/storage-services/service/rbc/rbpe/rbpe24/rbpe244/24404500/24404500.pdf.

2. "So God created mankind in his own image, in the image of God he created them; male and female he created them." (Gen 1:27).

we place our faith solely in ourselves and our government, to the exclusion of our personal and collective faith in God, we are ceding our real power to fallible man in a weak admission that it is the best we can do. We set ourselves up for perpetual disappointment or worse. The same holds true for both nation and faith: a house divided cannot stand.[3] No clearer example of this exists than the Civil War—the seeds of which were sown in an inherent tension between the utopian religious freedom ideals of Puritan New England and the secular profit motives of colonial Virginia and the South, where slavery fueled the economic engine.[4]

It took a war between the citizens of this nation to end slavery and unify the states. It cost more American lives by far than any other war in this nation's history. An estimated 620,000 soldiers died in battle—over the immorality of slavery.[5] Between battle deaths and disease, it is estimated that over 330,000 Union soldiers[6] died because they believed slavery, and its basis in racism and inequality, was wrong.

The Civil Rights Act of 1866 and the Fourteenth Amendment to the Constitution in 1868 were enacted shortly thereafter, giving citizenship to all African Americans and thus equal protection under the law, righting—legally and politically—a terrible wrong. While admittedly not dispositive of the racism and self-interest at the core of slavery (because secular law cannot change the human heart), these were not insignificant events. They were great manifestations of a sincere desire to change—to be better than we were.

Yet today a spiteful doctrine that attempts to redefine this nation, its history, and society as being *irreparably* racist called Critical Race Theory is being used to again divide the nation from within—*a house divided*. In an instant the deaths of all those people who sacrificed themselves for the cause of equality are summarily rendered irrelevant, and the struggle's historical significance along with it. When every other person and institution, indeed history itself, is cast as irremediably racist, no response is, or ever

---

3. Jesus said it himself: "If a kingdom is divided against itself, that kingdom cannot stand. If a house is divided against itself, that house cannot stand." (Mark 3:24–25).

4. As to this type of conflict, Jesus succinctly observed, "No one can serve two masters. Either you will hate the one and love the other, or you will be devoted to the one and despise the other. You cannot serve both God and money." (Matt 6:24).

5. See American Battlefield Trust, "Civil War Casualties," accessed at https://www.battlefields.org/learn/articles/civil-war-casualties.

6. See National Park Service, "Civil War Facts," accessed at https://www.nps.gov/civilwar/facts.htm.

will be, sufficient. The theory is designed to put a period at the end of the matter—to dismiss and exclude—itself hypocritically judgmental.

Racism exists. It lives on in self-interest and ignorance. There is no denying racism's historical significance or generational influence. Critical Race Theory is a specter of that influence. As applied by its advocates, however, the theory poses a problem without hope of solution. From a Christian perspective the theory ignores that exponentially larger problem of sin that subsumes, among countless evils, *any* prejudice or animus an individual may have toward another—for whatever reason. Racism is but one aspect of the sinful heart and the fallen human condition. We must therefore see the theory for what it is, a manufactured platform from which to promote and leverage not love and forgiveness but anger and discontent. Manipulated, the discontented fall prey to those seeking power. The real purpose of the theory is revealed in that manipulation and in the quest to shift power.

Sin, whatever form it takes, is not solved by secular legislation. Nor is it remedied by forced redefinition or indoctrination in media, education, business, or government—which is what the theory requires. We are currently witnessing that indoctrination being forced into our children's school curricula, our social and political institutions, and even our corporate culture. Sin is solely an issue of the heart which cannot be changed externally by indoctrination or force of law. Innate sin and its toxic effect on society and government could more accurately be titled Critical *Sin* Theory. As a major theme of this work, it offers a positive solution, one that boldly answers the sin of racism as well: the humility, love, mercy, and forgiveness of God, the creator of us all.

As God forgives all repentant sinners, racism—as with every indignation suffered at the hands of others—will never be truly remedied or healed until those who have suffered under it can forgive those who have subjected them to it, thereby placing ultimate judgment for those wrongs back into the hands of God—where it belongs. In forgiving those who have sinned against us, we free ourselves from the slavery of hate and the burden of that judgment to which we were bound. Only after forgiveness can we then begin to develop meaningful constructs for healing relationships and living in unity.

Unfortunately, the same forces that likewise strive to undermine that faith today are perpetually at work in undermining our unity as a nation. Destroy the former and you ultimately destroy the latter, preserving the disunity for those bent on exploiting it. This is why there is such a concerted effort by some in this nation to erase faith from the public domain. God is the true source of our individual and collective power. He is the foundation of this nation and its democracy, and the true source of its unity. By erasing faith, we erase the means by which we forgive each other for our past sins—just as God has forgiven us. Evil and disunity live on.

History proves that evil lives and that it is destructive. If left unopposed, evil will destroy us. We do not need to be told that totalitarianism in any worldly form is evil. The Nazi concentration camps and Russian pogroms revealed its horrors. China's oppression of human rights and religious freedom is evil, as is its desire for world dominion. Beheading infidels is evil. Slavery is evil—the ownership of another human being. Manipulating others is evil. Being forced to cede our individual liberties and property to a government for the sake of artificial economic and social equity is also evil. We have seen it, and are seeing it again in this country's progressive attempts to force the redistribution of wealth and in its support and promotion of a global one-world government. The censorship and indoctrination that result from those efforts is evil—a means of skewing perception—of stifling free speech and thought in order to quash social and political opposition. This list is endless.

We know where this all leads—to the death of democracy—a slow, subtle slide into a system where people are merely the expendable means to a political end. Apart from God's eternal rule, there is no such thing on this earth as a benevolent dictatorship. Nor should we endeavor to create one. To do so is to hasten the demise of our own freedom.

The growth and persistence of evil in our personal lives translates to the systemic evil within our society, our government, and hence the world. This is why external solutions to evil—the demand that "others change"— will never succeed. Like applying a bandage to cancer, it is absurdly inadequate. Rather than excising it, we merely cover it up. Sin, in all its forms, *is* systemic. It requires a systemic, internal solution, a means for the individual to deal with it inside themselves—a vaccine. When the systemic evil within society and government grows to that point where the people can no longer control it, it turns on us and usurps our individual freedom.

Pure freedom is to be like God. We all wish to be our own gods. How we choose to exercise that freedom will determine the state of this world. It is argued that God permits the existence of evil in this world as a clear choice between his perfection and our sin.[7] Freedom can be expressed

7. See Deut 30:19–20. God, speaking through Moses, told the Israelites:

either in love or in evil. For the believing Christian, this physical world is only a temporary accommodation, designed in part to reveal the nature of evil to those who would choose good, to those whose hearts are open to seeking the better, "more perfect" way. In choosing evil, we convict ourselves. But we are certainly free to do it. God seeks in the human heart love, humility, and personal accountability. The Spirit of God and God's perfect Prime Law provide the ability to exercise our freedom in love. Pursuing these ideals for the sake of God and one another benefits the relationships comprising our government.

Faith, in and of itself, does not change government. It fundamentally alters the hearts of its citizens and, in turn, their relationships with others. The quality of those relationships determines our understanding of democracy and the government which best expresses democracy's ideals. This is something that politics and law cannot do. They are only a reflection of those relationships.

As it is with the cause of Christ, despite highly visible platforms, that change will not come from biased or elite politics, media, law, or academia. Change will never come through the desire to leverage those platforms strictly for monetary, political, or professional gain. Just as it did for our revolutionary founders, it will come from the heart of the common person (*we the people*)—inspired by a humble God—a check and balance against the threat of tyranny. As such, this real potential for a fundamental change of heart, and the unity it inspires, makes it the most powerful force on earth—and the reason it is misunderstood, feared, and maligned.

This day I call the heavens and the earth as witnesses against you that *I have set before you life and death, blessings and curses. Now choose life* [emphasis added], so that you and your children may live and that you may love the Lord your God, listen to his voice, and hold fast to him. For the Lord is your life, and he will give you many years in the land he swore to give to your fathers, Abraham, Isaac and Jacob.

14

In The End

LOVE GOD—LOVE OTHERS as you love yourself.

That is God's Prime Law, a simple matter of the heart made infinitely more complex by matters of reason. Imperfect human reason has removed God's divinity as the power and authority behind that perfect Law. As wanderers in that age of reason, we seek truth everywhere except in the one place where God's divine Spirit and Law seek to dwell, our hearts—the home of government's real power.

Our national disunity thrives in that endless wandering—searching for the better deal—in seeking external political and social group solutions to issues comprising that disunity that, to this day, have all failed in uniting us because of our self-interest and lack of will. Anyone can espouse with best intentions social justice and grandiose systemic group social and political policy changes. Dusty bookshelves around the nation are stacked with such ideas. But without first changing the individual's internal will, there will be no lasting beneficial change.

As this writer painfully learned, in the end the key to finding that home is not patience, that things will change externally given time but, as it was for Job, humility—the humility to change internally and be accountable, first to God, then to one another. We must first be reconciled to God, as the ultimate source of our equality and freedom, before we can truly grasp and apply those ideals in reconciling our relationships with others. The dustiest book on that shelf is the only one pleading for that internal change, and it's the Law of God—the Bible. It is time to brush it off and give it a chance.

Like the Deist Ben Franklin at the Federal Convention, we can begin by seeking divine intervention through prayer. And like Job, for a time, alone with God, we must enter his perspective—to see ourselves for who and what we really are, weighing ourselves against a higher, perfect truth— a truth not of this world. Faith *is* the long process of applying that perfect truth to an imperfect life. So it is with an imperfect nation. We strive from generation to generation to apply God's perfection to the relationships comprising our democracy—constantly pushing forward, making it a bet- ter union by bettering ourselves, to the day when our stewardship ends and we discover with certainty what perfection truly is.

There is no true moral democracy without divine revelation. Our ability to fully understand and accept that revelation, and its effect on our understanding of ultimate morality, is realized through the Christian sal- vation experience. That process opens our hearts. It allows us to hear the spiritual and apply it properly, with accountability. Personal accountability and the willingness to submit in humility mark the true foundation of our moral democracy.

In that submission we acknowledge that our sin (imperfection) sepa- rates us from God and his perfect Law. That imperfection likewise separates us from each other. We muster the humility to request forgiveness for abus- ing the will God gave us—for breaking his Law. We accept the sacrifice made on our behalf by Christ to pay our debt for that abuse. We ask for and receive Christ (perfection) into our lives. We submit to his perfect love and try our best to incorporate it into all that we do. His love is our new authority. We pay that love forward each day thereafter.

These are the simple tasks of salvation. The transaction is simple, its effect profound. Christ has given us permission to rely on the power of God's Prime Law, first as it changes us (our will) individually, and then as it benefits our relationships with others. That truth was sealed upon Christ's resurrection and ascension to heaven—our guarantee of eternal life in a perfect realm.

Like the Apostle Paul on the road to Damascus, reconciling with God, we continue the journey of repairing our relationships with others as equals. Together, regardless of our pasts or differences, we are co-heirs with Christ[1] to the kingdom of God in which we are now equal, lawful citizens.

---

1. "Now if we are children [of God], then we are heirs—heirs of God and co-heirs

That is the revolutionary truth for which Christ died—a truth not of this world but made available to us all in the Word of God. In that truth is our salvation, individually and as a nation. From that salvation flows our ultimate freedom, for we are no longer slaves to that destructive imperfection. Unified by faith, we live a more perfect, more democratic life.

The Christian faith, if properly understood and applied, provides the power, the legitimacy, and the real strength behind our unique American democracy. It is the true source of our freedom, equality, and justice. It is the internal solution to our biggest external problem, giving us the strength to resist and counter evil in ourselves and, hence, our government. As the response to our tendency toward unbridled self-interest and the means of personal accountability, it is the vehicle through which God's power is made manifest in the people.

The founders who believed in that power, leveraged it by acknowledging the truth that as a people created in God's image, *we are free.* Though the form of our government permits the free expression of all faiths or none at all, without compulsion or interference, our freedom is not defined merely by the passive acknowledgment of a relationship between the individual and God. Nor is it defined in a desire to "rule" for the sake of power. It is defined in our love for and service to others—as equals.

Freedom and equality are not relative concepts. Nor are they strictly political or philosophical concepts. They are not merely social contractual quid pro quos for living peacefully with others, but rather innate attributes endowed upon us by our Creator, secured by all of us as acknowledged in our Constitution. They are transcendent rights. Their ultimate purpose is to effectuate God's perfect will for our lives. Freedom and equality as expressed in those rights are descriptors of our very essence, intrinsic attributes of our existence as beings created in God's image. For who is freer than God himself? And as his creations, there is only one freedom, one equality, and one justice applicable to us all individually and as a body politic.

If we understand that God's will for our lives is not fulfilled in slavery, however manifested, we will acknowledge our responsibility to promote and ensure freedom and to develop constructs to carry it out, for that is what God's love demands. This freedom is not realized by passively waiting for the government to respond and take control. It is asserted, fought for, maintained,

---

with Christ, if indeed we share in his sufferings in order that we may also share in his glory." (Rom 8:17).

and cherished. Freedom, like love, is work, for there will always be others lying in wait for opportunities to take advantage of our indifference.

Our nation's freedom was in many respects activated by our founders' signing of the Declaration of Independence. That freedom flowed from an act of unity against an oppressive authority. Likewise, our freedom from sin requires a unity of heart, ours and God's, for sin is an oppressive, enslaving authority. For many of those signers, the first battle for this nation's independence—the American Revolution—was fought in their own hearts when they acknowledged and repudiated their own sin, exchanging it instead for freedom in Christ. The Puritans and Pilgrims sought that same freedom when seeking a new home in this land. Of course, there was no greater revolutionary in history than Jesus Christ.

Today our freedom has fallen dormant in cynicism and apathy. We must rekindle that revolutionary Christian spirit and the freedom it embraces. Freedom is the responsibility to make decisions about one's life and one's government. Freedom is accountability for those decisions. In its progressive drift and mounting economic woes, our government has established itself as a perpetuator of self-victimization. Today's cults of political correctness and hypersensitivity are merely expressions of that victimization and sense of entitlement, our weak self-image, and our lack of trust.

And it shows. The government is the image of its people. Today, we appear to the rest of the world as a nation in debt financially, politically, and morally. We are heaping that debt upon the backs of our children—enslaving them in perpetuity—simply to satisfy ourselves in the present. We broadcast to the world an image of greed, hypocrisy, and weakness. Whoever controls the debt also controls the debtor. Our sin is no different. Whoever or whatever controls our sin also controls us.

We permit our great democracy to become enslaved by authoritarianism all in the name of a global economy, ignoring that in reconstructing the Tower of Babel,[2] the common language of globalism (money) consolidates greater power and wealth in fewer people. It is a head-long rush toward a one-world order, a faithless global dictatorship wielding power through a court with unlimited worldwide jurisdiction, one not bound by the terms of our unique Constitution and its protection of individual rights. As with both states and individuals in a true democracy, the value in decentralization of power is in preserving greater liberty among individual

2. See Gen 11:1–9.

sovereign nations and their citizens as a check and balance against that global dictatorship.

Government, be it local or global, is the cauldron where economic and moral debt are combined and stirred by sinful hands—in democracies and dictatorships alike. Reconnecting the two parts of God's Prime Law reestablishes in our hearts the bond between God's superior love and our love for others. It is the key to liberating ourselves from that debt. The strength of that bond is the divine morality of God's Law, personified in Jesus Christ who, at great expense, brought that truth to a sinful world. Maintaining that truth requires continued sacrifice. Through that sacrifice our founders envisioned this nation as a bastion of righteous strength and integrity, divine freedom and equality, and the hope of a better life through a better way.

Marring the unity of that vision, however, has been the battle within our own hearts between sin and righteousness, self and selflessness. There our decisions are made, our actions mapped out and implemented, and our words formed and given voice. There the war must be won. If not, the precious sacrifice of our patriots for the cause of freedom and equality will have all been in vain as we cede that hard-won freedom to a government that we no longer control.

Our founders and patriots did not die for a freedom leading to socialism or to some European clone or amorphous global union. Nor did they die for a freedom leading to mediocrity. They died for what this great nation represents: a body of righteous, free individuals with the heart of God, a God who willingly sacrificed himself as an expression of how much he values each one of us, and as an example of how to bear the burden of sacrificing ourselves for others. Therein God defined our precious stewardship of this great nation. In sacrificing our imperfect selves for others, we submit to the rule of law—of God *and* man. In that sacrifice, we become free.

That freedom is defined by its costs. Its ultimate cost is love. Despite faith's myriad detractors, that love is a currency the Christian God has in infinite supply. Once accepted and passed on, there is always more to take its place. The freedom and equality we enjoy in this wonderful democratic republic is best expressed in the ultimate freedom we have in the endless love and humility of Jesus Christ.[3]

---

3. "If you hold to my teaching, you are really my disciples. Then you will know the truth, and the truth will set you free." (John 8:31–32).

As it depends on us, it is an imperfect expression since we are imperfect. But our true home is in God's perfect immutable virtue and love which insulate us from being led astray by expedient or deceptive politics, or by those who would seek our subjugation. The unity that our nation so desperately needs this very day resides inside that love—the Spirit of God's Prime Law. It is the humble source of our incredible strength, both individually with God and together as a nation: one nation, under God, indivisible—truly a more perfect union.

Bibliography

American Battlefield Trust. "Civil War Casualties—The Cost of War: Killed, Wounded, Captured, and Missing." Updated January 26, 2023. https://www.battlefields.org/learn/articles/civil-war-casualties.

Arnold, Tyler, and Joe Bukuras. "FBI retracts leaked document orchestrating investigation of Catholics." *Catholic News Agency*, February 9. 2023. https://www.catholicnewsagency.com/news/253600/fbi-retracts-leaked-document-orchestrating-investigation-of-catholics.

Committee on Freedom of Expression. "Report of the Committee on Freedom of Expression." Chicago: University of Chicago, 2015. https://provost.uchicago.edu/sites/default/files/documents/reports/FOECommitteeReport.pdf.

Franklin, Benjamin. "Letter to Ezra Stiles." *The Works of Benjamin Franklin, Vol. XII Letters and Misc. Writings 1788–1790, Supplement, Indexes*, New York: G. P. Putnam's Sons, 1904. https://oll.libertyfund.org/titles/franklin-the-works-of-benjamin-franklin-vol-xii-letters-and-misc-writings-1788–1790-supplement-indexes.

Franklin, Benjamin. *The Autobiography of Benjamin Franklin*. 1771. The Federalist Papers Project, n.d. https://www.thefederalistpapers.org/wp-content/uploads/2012/12/The-Autobiography-of-Benjamin-Franklin-.pdf.

Galton, Francis. *Inquiries into Human Faculty and its Development*. London: Macmillan, 1883. https://cors.archive.org/details/inquiriesintohumoogalt/mode/1up?view=theater

Gopalakrishnan, Raju. "Exclusive: Council may rule Afghanistan, Taliban to reach out to soldiers, pilots." *Reuters*, August 18, 2021. https://www.reuters.com/world/asia-pacific/exclusive-council-may-rule-afghanistan-taliban-reach-out-soldiers-pilots-senior-2021-28-18/.

Harvard University. "Harvard Chaplains: Supporting Harvard students, faculty, postdoctoral researchers, and staff." 2018. https://chaplains.harvard.edu/about-harvard-chaplains.

Jefferson, Thomas. "Jefferson's Letter to the Danbury Baptists: The Final Letter, as Sent." *Library of Congress Information Bulletin* 57 (1998). https://www.loc.gov/loc/lcib/9806/danpre.html.

Justice, Tristan. "A Recap of NBC's Failed Attempt to Deplatform *The Federalist* on Google." *The Federalist*, June 22, 2020. https://thefederalist.com/2020/06/22/a-recap-of-nbcs-failed-attempt-to-deplatform-the-federalist-on-google/.

Bibliography

Kidd, Thomas S. *God of Liberty—A Religious History of the American Revolution*. New York: Basic Books, 2012.

Lewis, C. S. *Mere Christianity*. New York: Macmillan, 1952.

Lincoln, Abraham. "The Gettysburg Address." Speech, Gettysburg, PA, November 19, 1863. "Gettysburg address delivered at Gettysburg Pa. Nov. 19th 1863," The Library of Congress. PDF. Accessed May 26, 2023. https://tile.loc.gov/storage-services/service/rbc/rbpe/rbpe24/rbpe244/24404500/24404500.pdf.

Madison, James. *Debates in the Federal Convention of 1787*. 1787. Edited by Steve Straub, The Federalist Papers Project, n.d. http://www.thefederalistpapers.org/wp-content/uploads/2012/12/Debates-in-the-Federal-Convention-of-1787.pdf.

Milton, Michael A. *Foundations of a Moral Government—Samuel Rutherford's Lex, Rex. A New Annotated Version in Contemporary English*. Clinton: Tanglewood, 2019.

National Park Service. "Civil War Facts: 1861–1865." Updated October 27, 2021. https://www.nps.gov/civilwar/facts.htm.

Nietzsche, Friedrich Wilhelm. *Thus Spoke Zarathustra*. 1883. Cambridge Texts in the History of Philosophy. Edited by Adrian Del Caro and Robert Pippin. Translated by Adrian Del Caro. New York: Cambridge University Press, 2006.

NobelPrize.org. "Ivan Pavlov: Biographical." Nobel Prize Outreach AB 2023. Nobel Lectures, Physiology or Medicine 1901–1921. Amsterdam: Elsevier, 1967. https://www.nobelprize.org/prizes/medicine/1904/pavlov/biographical/.

Office of the Attorney General. "Partnership among Federal, State, Local, Tribal, And Territorial Law Enforcement to Address Threats against School Administrators, Board Members, Teachers, and Staff." Merrick Garland. Washington, DC: DOJ, October 4, 2021. https://www.justice.gov/ag/page/file/1438986/download.

Paine, Thomas. *The Age of Reason*. 1794–1807. USHistory.org, accessed April 27, 2023, https://www.ushistory.org/paine/reason/.

Planned Parenthood of Greater New York. "Planned Parenthood of Greater New York Announces Intent to Remove Margaret Sanger's Name from NYC Health Center." PlannedParenthood.org, July 21, 2020. https://www.plannedparenthood.org/planned-parenthood-greater-new-york/about/news/planned-parenthood-of-greater-new-york-announces-intent-to-remove-margaret-sangers-name-from-nyc-health-center.

Rousseau, Jean-Jacques. *The Social Contract: Or Principles of Political Right*. 1762. Edited by Jon Roland. Translated by G. D. H. Cole. Saylor.org, https://resources.saylor.org/wwwresources/archived/site/wpcontent/uploads/2012/09/POLSC2013.21.pdf.

Sartre, Jean-Paul. *No Exit, and Three Other Plays*. New York: Vintage International, 1989.

Tocqueville, Alexis de. "Unlimited Power of the Majority in the United States and Its Consequences." In *Democracy in America*, vol. 1. Translated by Henry Reeve. 1899. "Hypertexts," University of Virginia. https://xroads.virginia.edu/~Hyper/DETOC/1_ch15.htm.

US Treasury. "Major Foreign Holders of Treasury Securities." October 2022. https://ticdata.treasury.gov/Publish/mfh.txt.

Winthrop, John. "A Model of Christian Charity by Governor John Winthrop 1630." Edited by John Beardsley, The Winthrop Society. https://www.winthropsociety.com/a-model-of-christian-charity.